AF323760

THE SLAVS IN THE EYES OF THE OCCIDENT, THE OCCIDENT IN THE EYES OF THE SLAVS

THE SLAVS IN THE EYES OF THE OCCIDENT, THE OCCIDENT IN THE EYES OF THE SLAVS

EDITED BY
MARIA CIESLA-KORYTOWSKA

EAST EUROPEAN MONOGRAPHS, BOULDER
"UNIVERSITAS", KRAKOW

DISTRIBUTED BY COLUMBIA UNIVERSITY PRESS, NEW YORK

1992

EAST EUROPEAN MONOGRAPHS, NO. CCCLV

ISBN 0-88033-252-2

Printed in the United States of America

Preface

In November 1989, at the Jagiellonian University, an international symposium entitled ***The Slavs in the Eyes of the Occident, the Occident in the Eyes of the Slavs*** was held. The symposium was organized by the Polish Philology Institute of the Jagiellonian University. In this volume selected texts from the lectures delivered during the symposium by specialists in various fields are presented. This symposium was the third in a series of such events, the first of which was held in 1985 in Cracow (***Messianism and Slavophilism***, Cracow 1987), the second in 1987 in Bad Homburg; ***At the Origins of the Slav Cultures: Myths and Reality.***

Maria Cieśla-Korytowska

Contents

George P. Majeska — University of Maryland

Tsar'grad: The image of Byzatium in The Popular Lore of Medieval Russia

Byzantine influence in Russia has always been an important object of study for historians. Indeed even the world historian Arnold Toynbee has written on this topic. Most of this interest has focused on two basic questions: first, how Byzantium brought culture and civilization to (apparently barbaric) Rus': and second, how Byzantium served as a role model for Muscovy when it created an autocratic political system in the fifteenth and sixteenth centuries. The first focus emphasizes Byzantium's contribution to the formal, high culture of Russia (art, literature, religion, etc.) The second emphasizes the Russian adoption (or adaptation) of Byzantine (perhaps here better *byzantine* spelled with a small "b") political ideology in the time of Ivan the Great and Ivan the Terrible. These are indeed worthy topics, and they have gotten their due, if not their final evaluation.[1]

The focus of the present study, however, is somewhat different: it is the image of Byzantium in medieval Russia, particularly, the image of its capital.[2] The Russian image of the *Empire* has been effectively studied already as background to the theory of "Moscow the Third Rome", an idea that gained some currency in the fifteenth and sixteenth centuries. The fundamental content

---

1 A. T o y n b e e' s views on Byzantine influence in Russia are treated in his *A Study of History*[2], London 1948, I, pp. 17-26: for a critique of his ideas here see D. O b o l e n s k y, *Russia's Byzantine Heritage*, Oxford Slavonic Papers 1, 1950, pp. 37-63. O b o l e n s k y' s, *The Byzantine Commonwealth*, New York 1971, is an excellent presentation of the broad topic of Byzantine influence in Russia. More detailed studies include V. I k o n n i k o v, *Opyt' issledovanija o kul'turnom znaêenii Vizantii v russkoj istorii*, Kiev 1869, and F. T e r n o v s k i j, *Izuêenie vizantijskoj istorii i eja tendencioznoe priloženie v drevnej Rusi*, Kiev 1875-76. A recent assessment of the question of Byzantine influence in Russia, with up to date bibliography, is G. M a j e s k a, *Byzantine Influence on Russia*, Modern Encyclopedia of Russian and Soviet History VI, pp. 74-80.

2 The images of the Empire and its capital are inextricably intertwined in common parlance. Just as *Paris* equals *France* to foreigners, so Tsar'grad Constantinople equals the Byzantine Empire to the people of medieval Rus'.

of this theory was that Muscovy was the unique Christian state of eschatological significance, the only surviving divinely guided and guarded political entity. The imperial aura of *Roma aeterna* had somehow migrated from the banks of the Tiber to the shores of the Bosporus and finally (and with finality) to the bluffs overlooking the Moscow River. This vision of the God-protected city ruled by the divinely anointed sovereign reigning over the terrestrial icon of heaven is found regularly in the considerable body of tendentious "high-brow" literature extolling Moscow's new found place in history.[3] Slightly earlier, however, and less well studied by scholars, one can find a similarly exalted conception of Byzantium, albeit without the political pretensions and messianic tendencies projected onto emergent Moscow. Regular appeals to Byzantine practices as precedents and to Byzantine writings as unquestionable authorities were the basic elements of the debate between the Josephite party and its opponents, the Hesychast mystic Trans-Volga hermits, during the fifteenth-and sixteenth-century controversies about monastic landholding, treatment of heretics, etc. Their mode of argumentation betrays a tacit assumption by both groups that Byzantium was the ideal model of the divine order in this world.[4] Polemical literature, however, is probably not the best source for analyzing what Russians actually thought of Byzantium.

Most interesting should be the earliest impression of Constantinople among the Russians. The very name they gave the city, *Tsar'grad* ("the emperor's city") already suggests something of their early concept of Constantinople.[5] Telling elements of early Rus' "national myths" about Byzantium and its capital are also preserved in the early parts of the *Russian Primary Chronicle*, (the "Tale of Bygone Years"): however, the image of Constantinople that appears here is ambiguous. Constantinople is the marvelous trade emporium for trade with which the Viking and Russian princes are willing to go to war: it is a city so rich that one can leave it after a successful attack with sails made of

---

3 On Moscow as the "Third Rome" see the classic presentation by H. S c h ä d e r, *Moskau, das dritte Rom*[2], Darmstadt 1957, and more recently. A. L. G o l' d b e r g, *Ideja Moskva-tretij Rim*, Trudy Otdela Drevnerusskoj Literatury 37, 1983, pp. 139-49. A useful summary of the question, with bibliography is D. G o l d f r a n k, *Moscow, the Third Rome*, Modern Encyclopedia of Russian and Soviet History, XXIII, pp. 118-21.

4 This phenomenon is discussed in G. M a j e s k a, *Russia's Perception of Byzantium after the Fall*, The Byzantine Legacy in Eastern Europe, ed. L. Clucas. East European Monographs CCXXX, New York 1988, particularly pp. 27-29.

5 We have only random hints preserved in the sagas as to the concept of Constantinople. ("Miklagard") among the Viking warriors who opened up "the way from the Varangians to the Greeks".

silk.[6] It is also the city wherein during the Divine Liturgy one does not know whether one is "in heaven or on earth, for on earth is not such splendor or such beauty", as well as the "city guarded by God" which has lightning as its secret weapon and the special protection of the Mother of God who calls up storms to destroy enemy navies.[7] If the *Chronicle* seems to justify the Russians attacking Constantinople for commercial rights, it condemns Tsar Symeon of Bulgaria for attempting to conquer it[8]: he is, it would seem, challenging the natural order of things and thereby denying the legitimacy of Byzantine imperial rule. Despite the fact that the city and empire are of divine foundation, the Greeks who inhabit it are not necessarily portrayed positively in the Russian *Chronicle*. They are perfidious, treacherous and crafty, and the chronicler lists some convincing examples of why he thinks "the Greeks are deceivers to the present day".[9] Yet when the same chronicler searches for material to use in economia for the chief heroes of his tale, those who brought Christianity to Rus': he reverts to describing Olga as the "new Helen ... worthy to rule" along with the emperor in Constantinople.[10] The Russian chronicler can apparently think of no higher political honor to which a ruler could aspire than emperor of Byzantium. Thus it is the Byzantine imperial house that regularly serves as the basis for metaphors of powerful rules. Vladimir the Christianizer of Russia, is accounted "the new Constantine of mighty Rome who baptized himself and his subjects, for the Prince of Rus' imitated the deeds of Constantine himself."[11] The "mighty Rome" here is, of course, "New Rome", Constantinople.

Interestingly, at about the same time that the Chronicle was being put in final form. Metropolitan Hilarion of Kiev, a native Russian whose appointment to the Russian metropolitanate caused difficulties with the Constantinopolitan Mother Church, eulogized the same Prince Vladimir as "Baptizer of the Rus'" while downplaying the role of "New Rome" and the Empire in his famous "Sermon on Law and Grace". He compares the Russian saint not to Emperor Constantine in the first instance, but to the very apostles who brought the light of Christian faith to various lands. He names several of the missionary apostles along with their mission territories, but the Apostle Andrew's visitation of Constantinople is not on the list, albeit the author eventually must note that

---

6 *Povest Vremennyx let*, Polnoe Sobranie Russkix Letopisej[12], Leningrad 1926, cols. 29-38, pp. 44-45.

7 Ibid., cols. 21-22, 45, 108.

8 Ibid., col. 43.

9 Ibid., 30,70.

10 Ibid., 60-61.

11 Ibid., 130-31.

Vladimir had heard of the "Christ-loving noble Greek land, strong in faith" where miracles and signs occur.[12] Only later in the sermon is Vladimir described as "equal in mind, love of Christ and honor" to "Constantine the Great" in his establishing of the institutions of the Christian Church in his land.[13] Once more we have ambivalence about Tsar'grad particularly when we learn in the same sermon that Vladimir's capital city of Kiev is under the protection of the Mother of God, just as Constantinople is, although this latter fact remains unmentioned.[14]

Both the *Primary Chronicle* and Hilarion's sermon are, in a sense, official documents that reflect the publicly espoused views of the élite of Kievan Rus': the politically aware. Less oriented toward possible political motives are Lives of Saints. This more popular genre provides some insight into "middle-level" Russian images of Constantinople in early Rus': *The Kiev Caves Patericon* (an essentially thireenth-century collection of Lives of Monks of this monastery along with stories from the monastery's history) manifests several different images of Constantinople. The Byzantine capital is for example, the center of Christian artistic production *par excellence*. Architects and painters are sought there to decorate the monastery's sanctuaries, and they are even dispatched from thence to Rus' by miraculous means.[15] The founder of the community, the ascetic Anthony, went to "Constantine's city" to become a monk, but apparently did not find there the kind of monastic life he sought. He continued on to the monastic community of Mount Athos and there was tonsured, bringing to the most important monastery of ancient Rus' "the blessing of the Holy Mountain"[16], rather than of the Byzantine capital. His eventual successor, Theodosius, considered the second founder of the monastery, however, introduced the cenobitic monastic order to the community by accepting the rule of the Constantinople Studite Monastery[17], Constantinopolitan monasticism seems to have replaced Athonite as the model to be imitated.

---

[12] *Des Metropoliten Ilarion Lobrede auf Vladimir den Heiligen*. ed. L. Müller, Slavistische Studienbücher II, Wiesbaden 1962, pp. 99-107, 109. The editor, ibid., 24-28, argues against an anti-Greek bias in the work.

[13] Ibid., 117-20.

[14] Ibid., 123-24. On the tradition of the Mother God as protector of Constantinople see N. H. B a y n e s. *The Supernatural Debenders of Constantinople*, Analecta Bollandiana 67, 1949, pp. 167-77; reprined in his *Byzantine Studies and Other Essays*, London 1955, pp. 248-60.

[15] *Das Paterikon des Kiever Höhlenklosters nach der Ausgabe von D. Abramovic*, ed.D. Tschižewskij Slavische Propyläen 2, Munich 1964, pp. 5-10, 172.

[16] Ibid., 16.

[17] Ibid., 39.

The case is somewhat different in the early fifteenth-century Life of St. Sergius of Radonezh written by Epiphanius the Wise (and edited by Pachomius the Logothete ["the Serb"]). Here the concept of Constantinople plays varied roles, most notably as a basis for comparision with Russia in matters of sanctity, and again, as source of authority. Sergius was a self-appointed hermit, born, the *Vita* notes, under "the pious, most celebrated, powerful Tsar Andronicus [II], the Greek autocrat who ruled in *Tsar'grad* under the Archbishop of Constantinople Callistos, the Ecumenical Patriarch", as well as (as an afterthought?) under the Russian Grand Prince Dmitry of Tver and under Metropolitan Peter of All Rus'.[18] The *Vita* recounts the wonders of Sergius' pious life, made all the more remarkable, the author notes, by the fact that Sergius "lived in our days, times and years, in our own country" (that is to say, in Russia) and that he "did not visit *Tsar'grad* nor the Holy Mountain [Athos], nor Jerusalem", as did the author[19] (who did not become an important saint). Still, the author of the *Vita* tells us serval times, the fame of Sergius' sanctity reached "even *Tsar'grad* and Jerusalem".[20] As proof of this statement, the reader is told, for example, that a bishop from Constantinople who was visiting Mocsow came to see Sergius at his rustic retreat and exclaimed, "How can it be that in these countries such a light appeared?". The metaphor of the light was very apt because God blinded that haughty Byzantine chauvinist: Sergius, however, cured him[21]. It is a fact that Sergius' fame reached even to Constantinople, for Patriarch Philotheus of Constantinople was moved to write the hermit, complimenting him on his holiness of life and then ordering him to introduce cenobitic monastic life in his heretofore loosely regulated community. The response of the Russian saint to the patriarchal ukase is instructive. He went to the Russian metropolitan in Moscow to ask if it had to be obeyed. It did, replied Metropolitan Alexis, the most astute politician of fourteenth century Russia.[22] Even saints are no longer as sure as Theodosius once was that Constantinople was the arbiter of the faith.

All of the material cited heretofore is literary, that is, written, and thus represents works that emanated from the literate classes of Old Russia, most

---

18 *Žitie prepodobnogo i bogonosnogo otca našego Sergija čudotvorca* ed. Archim. Leonid, Pamjatniki drevnej pis'mennosti i iskusstva 58, St. Petersburg 1885, pp. 22. On the possible relationships between the preserved texts of this work see ibid., I-XVIII and *Die Legenden des Heiligen Sergij von Radonez Nachdruck der Ausgabe von Tichonravov*, ed. L. Müller, Slavische Propyläen 17, Munich 1967, I-XII.

19 *Žitie otca našego Sergija*, 159 Encomium.

20 Ibid., 135. 150 et al.

21 Ibid., 135.

22 Ibid., 106-07.

notably from the clergy. The clergy are, of course, the group most exposed to the image of the Byzantine capital in written material, particularly the liturgical texts of the Orthodox Chruch, which have a very strong Constantinopolitan, not to say Byzantine, bias. But ther literate, both clergy and educated laymen, formed a very small portion of the medieval Russian populace. The best source for what "the rest of the Russians" thought of Constantinople and Byzantium is popular, oral literature, that is, folklore. Folklore, however, is dangerous to use as historical evidence. It is extremely diffucult to date a specific detail in a piece of folk literature. One makes an "act of faith" that folklore is an essentially conservative genre and hopes that one's conclusions are not horrendously skewed by the peculiar propensities of the collector one is forced to depend on.

With these caveats in mind, a brief analysis of folklore thought to date from the middle ages might be in order. Non-narrative types of Russian folklore (seasonal and ceremonial songs, lamentations, riddles, charms and proverbs[23]) seem to say nothing about Constantinople. The case is similar for the folk tale, the Russian equivalent of the fairy tale: an admittedly cursory reading of the texts in the standard collection of Russian folk tales (which contains some six hundred tales) comes up with no mention of *Tsar'grand* or a variant thereof at all.[24] It would thus seem that Constantinople (or the Byzantine Empire) is not a folk tale element of any consequence. The reason cannot be that these tales all predate the introduction of Christianity in Russia, for they abound in churches, icons, signs of the cross, priests and deacons and, in fact, they borrow motifs from lives of saints. *Tsar'grad* is simply not part of Russia's fairy-tale world, perhaps because these works hark back to a period before there was any contact between Byzantium and the Eastern Slavs.

Studying the byliny, the "folk epics" of old Rus', oral poetic songs dealing with heroes and battles is a slightly more rewarding endeavor for those interested in the popular Russian view of Byzantium. The earliest known collection of *byliny*, the large set gathered in Siberia in the mid-eighteenth century by Kirsha Danilov, contains three references to "Tsar'grad". In the *bylina* "Nightingale Budimirovich" there is twice talk of "*Tsar'grad* tricks" (xitrosti byli Carja-grada)[25], while in another bylina the hero Stavr the Boiar

---

23 On these folklore genres in Russia, as on the relationship of folk literature to historical events, see I. M. S o k o l o v, *Russian Folklore* with a preface by F. Oinas Hatboro Pa. 1966 and D. K. Z e l e n i e n *Russische (ostslavische) Volkskunde*, Berlin 1927.

24 A. N. A f a n a s' e v, *Narodnye russkie skazki*, ed. L.G. Barag and N.V. Novikov, 3 vols., Moscow 1984.

25 *Drevnie rossijskie stixotvorenija sobrannye Kirševu Danilovym*, ed. A.P. Evgen'eva and B.N. Putilov, Moscow 1958, pp. 10, 11 (and also *Jerusalem wise thoughts* [mudrosti Ierusalimal]).

entertains at a heroic banquet by playing a "Tsar'grad tune".[26] A song recorded in a later collection preserves the Constantinopolitan musical connection when the hero Dobrinja plays a song from *Tsar'grad* and a song from Jerusalem before singing his own song.[27] Elsewhere Dobrinja plays a *gusli* (a Russian folk instrument), which has three strings: one from Kiev, one from *Tsar'grad*, and one from Jerusalem.[28] These references to the imperial city of Byzantium are rarities, however and play only a minor role in the Russian world of epic myth. A much more common Byzantine prop in the *byliny* is the "wide-brimmed hat of the Greek land", a cap normally worn by pilgrims, and thus a common disguise for epic heroes in trouble. This "hat of the Greek [i.e., Byzantine] land", sometimes described as "the saracen hat of the Greek land"[29], has magic properties. The hero Dobrinja uses it to stun the dragon Gorynchisha when caught bathing naked and unarmed in a river[30]. In another version the hat is not so magical: Dobrinja has to fill it with sand to make it effective[31]. But in any case, Byzantine artifacts would seem to possess a degree of supernatural power.

On occasion, at least, the city of Constantinople itself appears in *byliny*. Usually it is simply a far-away place from which, fairy tale fashion, a hero rushes back to save his fiancée from marrying another.[32] Somewhat more historically, the *bylina* called "Ilija and Idolishche" has the Russian hero Ilija Muromets journeying to Tsar'grad and attacking and killing the Tatar monster Idolishche ("Little idol"), who has conquered the city, taken Tsar Constantine prisoner, and destroyed the holy icons[33]. The "little Tatar idol" doubtless stands for the Constantinople in 1453 and installed Islam with its distaste for sacred images. Elsewhere the *bylina* tradition records a trip by a less heroic Ilija Murometr to *Tsar'grad* : this time he is disguised as a pilgrim and people have to appeal to

---

26 *Sygriš sygral Carja-grada*, ibid., 96 (he also does *Jerusalem dances*).

27 *Onežskie byliny zapisannye A.F. Gil'ferdingom*, vol. 3, ed. A.I. Nikiforov & G.S. Vinogradov, Moscow 1940, pp. 160.

28 Ibid., 440-41. In another version, his *gusli* is said to be tuned in three keys for the same cities, Ibid., 17.

29 *Stixotvorenija sobrannye Kirševu Danilovym*. 127-28. The actual collected texts often read "*Sorochinsk* hat of the Greek land" confusing the unfamiliar word *saracen* with the more familiar famous fair town of nineteenth-century Russia.

30 *Stixotvorenija, sobrannye Kirševu Danilovym*. 236-37.

31 *Onežskie byliny* p. 406.

32 *Onežskie byliny*, Vol. 2, ed. A.I. Nikiforov, Moscow 1938, pp. 484, 486; Dobrinja seems to have been there playing cards, ibid., 488, although other *byliny* have him besieging the city for three years twice (*Onežskie byliny*, vol. 3, pp. 11, 112).

33 One*žskie byliny*, Vol. 3, pp. 240-45; cf. 8-11.

Tsar Constantine because of a row he causes in a tavern.[34] At least one bylina is actually set in "Tsar'grad", the bylina of "Tsar Solomon and Vasilij Okolovich", which recounts how Tsar Vasilij Okulovich", of *Tsar'grad* has Solomonida, the wife of Tsar Solomon Davidovich of Jerusalem, abducted in order to wed her. It ends with Tsar Solomon outwitting Tsar Vasilij and taking "all *Tsar'grad* captive".[35] In the end, however, byliny references to Tsar'grad are very rare and full of anachronisms, and *Tsar'grad* is in no way central to the mythic landscape of the Russian folk epic.

One would expect a more sophisticated and articulated image of Byzantium, the capital of the Eastern Christian world, in the "sacred songs", the stixi duxovnye, sung originally by Russian pilgrims and later by wandering bands of religious beggars (kaleki-perexožie).[36] These wanderers appear as characters in byliny and have probably been around a long time. Many of their songs are based on popular Lives of Saints (e. g., the Life of St. Alexis the Man of God) or are created on the slight frame of a well known saint's Life such as that of St. George the Great Martyr (George the Brave, son of St. Sophia who lived under Tsar Diocletian [or "Tsar Theodore Stratilate"] and fought "the Moslems"[!].[37] Other "sacred songs" are based on biblical, particularly New Testament, themes or on church festivals.[38] Needless to say, many of these songs have their genesis in written material. For any discussion of the Russian vision of Constantinople, the most interesting of the songs of these Russian "Christian troubadours" is one included, in seventeen versions of varying length, in the basic collection of sacred songs, compiled by Peter Kireevsky. It is called the

---

34 Ibid., 148-50; another *bylina* records the incident as happening in Halicz, ibid., 261-64.

35 *Pesni sobrannyja P.N. Rybnikovym*, vol.2, Moscow 1910, pp. 556-65. A different version in the same collection ibid., 273, makes Tsar Vasilij ruler of the Kingdom of "Kudrija" (Carstvo Kudrijanskoe) white a related song names no kingdom for Tsar Vasilij: see ibid, vol. 1, Moscow 1909, pp. 469-79.

36 Just what their wandering life is like is suggested by the high spirited *bylina* "Sorok kalik so kalikoju"(forty wanderers plus one). *Stixotvorenija, sobrannye Kiršeju Danilovym.* 155-65. et al. On the tradition of these wandering pilgrims see I. S r e z n e v s k i j, *Russkie kaliki drevnego vremeni*, Zapiski Imperatorskoj Akademii Nauk 1. fasc. 2, 1862, pp. 186-210. In one of thier songs the band claims that its fraternity was founded at Christ's ascension; see P. B e s s o - n o v, *Kaleki perexožie*, 2 vols. in 6 fasc, Moscow, pp. 1861-64, I, 1-7. On the genre of stixi duxovnye (spiritual songs) see ibid. II I-XIVIII and A. V e s e l o v s k i j, *Razyskanija v oblasti russkix duxovnyx stixov*, St. Peterburg, 1879-1891.

37 B e s s o n o v. I, pp. 97-154; 393-504; sometimes George the Brave fights the "Latins" rather than the Moslems, ibid., 405.

38 Ibid., vol. II.

"Golubinaja kniga", the "book of the dove".[39] It is essentially mumbo-jumbo revolving around questions posed to the "Wise Tsar David Evseevich" by the rulers of the world, particularly "Tsar Vladimir Vladimirovich", apparently meant to be Prince Vladimir the Christianizer of Rus', or Prince Vladimir Monomach of Kiev, or both together. A study of the mystifications of this work suggests why *Tsar'grad* plays so small a part in Russian folklore collected in modern times. One learns from the *Golubinaja kniga* for instance, that the "Mother of All Cities" is Jerusalem because in the middle of Jerusalem there is a church, in the middle of the church there is a white marble casket, and in the white marble casket is the robe of Christ.[40] Here is our Tsar'grad, for the robe of Christ was not preserved in Jerusalem in the middle ages, but in Constantinople where it played an important role in establishing Constantinople's credentials as a holy city.[41] Constantinople, the sacred capital of the Christian Empire, has, it seems, at least occasionally, been amalgamated in the folk imagination with Jerusalem, the sacred city of the Holy Scripture.

Those reciting the *Book of the Dove* might also be confusing Jerusalem/ *Tsar'grad* with Moscow, however, one of the most sacred relics to make its way to Mocsow was precisely the "robe of Christ". This precious relic came to the Muscovite tsar from Georgia as a gift of the Shah of Persia and might be a garment of Christ that was taken from Constantinople by the Turks during the sack of the city in 1453. Perhaps it was even the relic of Christ's robe that had served as a palladium of the Byzantine capital when it was kept at the Blachernae shrine in Constantinople. Whichever garment of Christ it was, the sacred robe was ceremoniously received by Tsar Michael Fedorovich in 1625, and Patriarch Philaret of Moscow and All Rus' publicly enshrined in a casket in the middle of the Dormition Cathedral of the Moscow Kremlin in the middle of the city of Moscow. That momentous event was commemorated by an annual holiday in the Russian Church celebrated on 10 July.[42] This sacred garment of Christ thought to have earlier graced the imperial palace Pharos Church of the Mother

---

39 The title might also be taken to mean "the deep book". Various versions are published ibid., I, pp. 269-378.

40 B e s s o n o v I. pp. 271, 276, et al. Sometimes the "Church of the Mother of God" is also identified as the Church of the Resurrection (i.e., the Church of the Holy Sepulchre) and its relic is the tomb of Christ: cf. ibid., p. 295.

41 Christ's robe was shown in the Pharos Church of the Mother of God at the imperial palace Constantinople until the sack of the city by the crusaders, and later at the Constantinopolitan shrines of Blachernae and Chalcoprateia; see J. E b e r s o l t, *Sanctuaires de Byzance,* Paris 1921, pp. 44-60, 116-120.

42 V.N. I v a n o v, *Moskovskij Kreml,* Moscow 1971, 82 and T.V. T o l s t a j, *Uspenskij Sobor moskovskogo kremlja,* Moscow 1979, pp. 37-38 and pl. 14.

of God in Constantinople and the Blachernae Church of the Mother of God, the robe that had so much to do with saving Constantinople from barbarian attacks, now rested in the palace church of the Muscovite tsars. Moscow, to judge from the singers of the sacred songs, had thus become the new Christian "Tsar'grad" ("the emperor's city"). The "sacred songs" give further evidence to support this analysis. One learns from the *Golubinaja kniga* that the "Tsar of Tsars" is the "White Tsar"[43] — that is, the Russian ruler. "He is Tsar of Tsars because he believes in the baptized and pious Orthodox faith, the Mother of God, and the Undivided Trinity, and he stands for the house of the Mother of God", the song explains.[44] The "house of the Mother of God" for which the Russian tsar stands is, of course, the Cathedral of the Dormition of the Mother of God in the Moscow Kremlin, the cathedral of the primate of Russia, the coronation church of the Muscovite tsars, and — the church in the middle of which stands a casket which holds the robe of Christ. This shrine in the Kremlin palace of the Muscovite tsars, that is, of the Muscovite emperors, is thus a new Blachernae Church, a Muscovite version of the shrine of the Mother of God that had protected Constantinople ("New Rome") and which now protected the Third Rome. The "White Tsar" of Muscovy hence becomes "the Tsar of Tsars", a role one would have assigned to the vice-gerant of God, emperor of Constantinople before the destruction of the Byzantine Empire.

The concept of *Tsar'grad* plays, then serval roles in Russian folklore. The *Tsar'grad*-Byzantine Empire of the *byliny* was a metaphor for a faraway exotic realm whence came exotic music and magic pilgrim hats, but it was also a land where a dreadful monster appeared to destroy the holy icons, i.e., to persecute the Orthodox faith. In the sacred songs, however, this persecution of the Orthodox faith in Byzantium seems to have destroyed the numenous status of the city and attributes of the sacred city of Constantinople were transferred to the biblical holy City of Jerusalem. When the rulers of Muscovy asserted their claim to be the consecrated Orthodox Christian emperors in succession to Byzantium[45], the singers of the "sacred songs" assigned various aspects of the sacred imperial heritage of Constantinople-subsumed-under-Jerusalem to Mo-

---

43 B e s s o n o v I. 271 et al. The terminology "white tsar" is of Mongol derivation and is applied to the Lord of Muscovy only in the fifteenth century at the earliest: see G. V e r n a d s k y, *The Mongols and Russia,* A History of Russia, III, New Haven 1953, pp. 388-89.

44 B e s s o n o v I, pp. 271, 276, et al.

45 Cf. M. C h e r n i a v s k y, *The Reception of the Council of Florence in Moscow,* Church History 24, 1955, pp. 347-59.

scow. Moscow became not only the third Rome, but thereby also the new New Jerusalem. By extension, then, Russia became a new version of the Holy Land.[46] The "Book of the Dove" seems to reflect this transfiguration of Rus' into the promised land when it answers the question: "What lake is the mother of lakes?" thus: "Lake Il'men is the mother of all lakes, not the Il'men that is near Novgorod, but the Il'men that is in the Turkish land, the Il'men that lays near Jerusalem: it is from this Il'men lake that flows out little mother River Jordan."[47] The numernous image of Tsar'grad so clearly preached in the liturgical readings of the Orthodox Church has not been lost in Russian popular lore; it has been absorbed and reinterpreted to fit later times, as so often happens in folklore.

---

[46] Cf. Ibid., *Holy Russia: A Study in the History of an Idea*, American Historical Review, 63, 1958, pp. 617-37.

[47] Bessonov, I, p. 295.

Tsuguo Togawa — Sophia University, Tokyo

The Japanese View on Russia Before and After the Meiji Restoration

Togawa Tsuguo[1]

In this report I would like to shed a new light upon the classic theme of "Russia and Europe" from the viewpoint of the modernization of late comers. Both Russia and Japan started the process of modernization in the middle of the 19th century, later than the countries of Western Europe: in Russia the great reforms under Alexander II, and in Japan the Restoration of Meiji of 1867. In both cases the start was made by the Western impact, and the modernizing process was led by the governments.[2]

Russia and Japan had long cultural traditions, and the introduction of Western value systems caused a lot of conflicts within the societies. Among those who insisted on the necessity of maintaining the traditional values, there was a tendency to attribute a higher spiritual value to their own culture, although they had to admit the supremacy of the Western material civilization. In Russia, needless to say, the Slavophiles represented those opinions.

In Japan, in the first half of the 19th century, a new slogan coined by a thinker named Sakuma Shozan (1811-1864) had a great influence upon Japanese intellectuals of the samurai class. This slogan, in Japanese, was "tōyō dōtoku, seiyō geijutu": that is to say, the East is superior in morals, the West is superior in science.[3] To be sure, there were quite a few nationalists and admirers of the West as well at that time, but the reconciliation of two values which was expressed in that slogan seemed to become the main Japanese attitude after the Meiji Restoration.

---

1 In this report, all Japanese names are shown according to Japanese usage: the family names first, and then given names.

2 cf. B l a c k. C.E.,ed.,*The Modernization of Japan and Russia: a Comparative Study,* N.Y./,1975.

3 Matsumoto S a n n o s u k e, *Sakuma Shōzan,* Nihon no shisōka (Japanese Thinkers), vol.1, Asahi Shimbun-sha, 1962, pp. 20-36. (The Japanese phrase is also rendered: *Eastern ethics, Western technique.*)

Before and after the Restoration, the Japanese government sent many young people to West European countries and the United States, and also invited Western specialists in various fields: strategy, navigation, medical science, agriculture, law, philosophy, literature, fine arts and so forth. We can say that the number of students sent to each country shows the degree of interest of the government in each of them. Immediately after the Restoration, from 1870 to 1871, 149 students went to the United States, 126 to England, 66 to Germany, 42 to France, but to Russia only 9, including 3 who went with the Iwakura Embassy, which I will talk about later.[4]

Before the Restoration, the Tokugawa shogunate had sent six young samurai to the Russian capital with the recommendation of the first Russian Consul, Iosif Goshkevich. After the collapse of the shogunate, they all returned home except one, Ichikawa Bunkichi, who later became professor of Russian at The Tokyo Institute of Foreign Languages. Although most of the students sent abroad by the government before and after the Restoration had distinguished careers in Meiji Japan, few of those who studied in Russia succeeded later. Among the nine just mentioned, the only great success was Nishi Tokujirō (1847-1912), sent by the Meiji government to the Faculty of Law of the University of St. Petersburg, who became later Minister of Foreign Affairs. This suggests not only the comparative inability of the students but also the low evaluation of Russia by the government. It regarded Russia as a country less advanced than the other Western states, and thought study in the Russian Empire of little use.

*

In 1869 (the second year of Meiji), a governmental organ "Meiji Gekkan" (Monthly Magazine of Meiji) classified countries of the world in the following five categories. (1) Civilized Countries (bunmei no kuni): England, France, Holland, U.S.A. (Such countries as Austria, Prussia, Denmark, and Sweden will soon belong to this category). (2) Enlightened countries (kaika no kuni): Russia, Italy, Spain, Portugal, and countries of Latin America. (3) Half-enlightened countries (hankai no kuni): China, India, Turkey, Persia, and African countries north of Sahara. (4) Countries of uncivilized manners and customs (izoku no kuni): nomadic tribes in Siberia, Central Asia, Arabia, and Africa. (5) Barbarians

---

4 Togawa T s u g u o, *Iwakura shisetsu-dan to roshia* (The Iwakura Misson and Russia), Bulletin of the Faculty of Foreign Studies, No.23, Sophia University, pp.133-174.

(yaban): American Indians, natives of Africa and Australia.[5] In the press published at that time, such a classification was very common; and the idea of progress from a barbarian to a civilized country became very popular not only among the intellectuals but also among the common people. Such an idea was expressed by the governmental slogan "bunmei kaika" (civilization and enlightenment). Another slogan promoted by the government was "fukoku kyohei" (enrich the nation and strengthen the army), which, I think, was similar to propaganda of the Russian, Turkish, and some other governments of late comers.

*

Both continuity and change can be found in the Japanese evaluation of Russia from before until after the Meiji Restoration. The continuity consists of two opposite views on Russia in connection with her advance toward Japan. In the 1780s two essays appeared after the first Russian visit to northern Japan. In one entitled "Akaezo Fusetsu-kō" (A Study of Red Ainu [i.e.Russian] Reports), the author,Kudo Heisuke (1734-1800), attributed to the Russians primarily a commercial aim and denied the Russian menace. He said that it was a rumor made by the Dutch, who wished to keep a monopoly on trade with Japan. The other, with the title of "Kaikoku Heidan" (Military Discussion Regarding the Maritime Nation), was written by Hayashi Shihei (1738-93), who warned against Russian encroachment in the north and even the possibility of a Russian attack on Japan. Both Hayashi and Kudō made their studies of Russia after the Japanese translation of Dutch works on Russian history and geography.[6] So, from the beginning, the Japanese view on Russia was influenced by a third country which did not like Japan's friendly relationship with Russia. And those two opposite views on Russia have continued for a long time, in a sense, even up to the present.

Next to Holland, from the middle of the 19th century to the beginning of the 20th, it was England which had a dominant influence upon the Japanese view on Russia; and from the end of World War II, the United States has been affecting Japan's view on Russia and the Soviet Union.[7]

---

5 Yamamuro S h i n i c h i, *Dokono kuni ni manabuka* (Which Country Should We Study?) Kaigai shiten nihon no rekishi (Japanese History From the Viewpoint of Abroad), vol.13, Gyosei, 1986, p. 51.

6 Tsuguo T o g a w a, *Slavistika v Iaponii*, Obozrenie, No. 8, Paris, 1984, pp. 26-30.

7 Togawa T s u g u o, *Nichiro nisso kankei to daisan-koku no kainyu* (The Interventions of third countries in Russo-Japanese and Soviet-Japanese Relations), Fukase T a d a k a z u, et al., eds., Hokkaido de heiwa o kangaeru (Considering Peace in Hokkaido), Hokkaido University Press, 1988, pp. 83-98.

There was also an undeniable change of evaluation of Russia. In the first half of the 19th century, among the Japanese intellectuals there were some who paid special attention to Peter the Great and admired his achievements.

Sakuma Shozan, for example, wrote in 1838 about the transformation of Russia under Peter the Great: before Peter, Russia was very poor and bullheaded, but Peter made her "one of the most honorable countries in Europe". In the same year Watanabe Kazan (1793-1841), one of the leaders of westernization, also mentioned Peter's great works: construction of new capital, military victories, extension of territory, education of the nation, invitation of foreign specialists, and making Russia "the first empire of the world". Watanabe emphasized that all those great works were accomplished in a generation, and suggested that Japan should follow this example.[8]

It should be mentioned that, at the end of the Edo period, Russia was regarded as both a "northern menace" and as a "country of justice" (gikoku).In the mid-1850s, the Tokugawa shogunate was forced to conclude a series of "unequal treaties" with the Western powers. The American fleet under Commodore Perry first came to Edo (Tokyo) Bay, neglecting the traditional Japanese regulation by which all foreign vessels had to enter Nagasaki. On the other hand, the Russian fleet under Admiral Putiatin came to Nagasaki and negotiated with a Japanese delegation with great patience. A Russian novelist, Ivan Goncharov (1812-91) who visited Nagasaki as secretary to Putiatin, wrote about friendly relations between two representatives in his "Russians in Japan at the beginning of 1853 and at the end of 1854". Therefore, is is not without reason that the Meiji government later decorated Putiatin with a first rank order.

Putiatin was the third Russian envoy to Japan: the first was Adam Laksman, sent by Catherine II; and the second was Nikolai Rezanov, sent by Alexander I. Both of them did not try to resort to force, but obeyed Japanese law and customs. They even brought with them some Japanese castaways, which made a good impression on the Japanese people. That is the reason why Russia was called a "country of justice" at that time.[9]

However, that high evaluation of Russia was to change because of two reasons. The first was Japanese study of the real circumstances of Russia, and the second was the influence of the British Russophobia.

---

8 Wada H a r u k i, *Predstavlenie o Rossii v Iaponii; uchiter' ,vrag,sobrat po stradaniam*, Latyshev, I. A., ed., Rossia i Iaponia v issledovaniakh sovetskikh i iaponskikh uchenykh, Moskva, 1986, pp. 50-61.

9 Togawa T s u g u o, *Wakaki Mori Arinori no roshia kan a meguette* (The young Mori Arinori's view on Russia), Slavic Studies, No. 32, Hokkaido University, 1985, pp. 81-82.

*

As to the change in the evaluation of Russia, we can see a good example in the diary of the young Mori Arinori (1847-99)[10], who later established the basic systems of modern education as first Minister of Education. While he was studying as a student at the University College of the University of London, he visited St. Petersburg in the summer of 1866. Shortly after his arrival at Kronstadt, he was advised never to talk about politics in Russia. He was astonished to be offered cigarettes by a Russian officer on board his ship in spite of the strict regulation against smoking in the port. From this experience the young student learned of the hypocrisy of Russian officialdom, and the contradiction between principle and reality in Russia.

Looking at many ships in the port, Mori described the situation of Russian commerce and trade. Using British materials, he wrote that Russian exports were slightly more than half of her imports, and came to the conclusion that Russia was incompetent at commerce. However, the figures which he cited in his diary were not reliable and neither was his conclusion.

During his stay in the Russian capital, he was much impressed by the people's reverence for the Tsar, and gained the impression that the Russian autocracy was completely different from the British political system and resembled rather the Japanese and Chinese imperial systems. At the same time, he wrote that after the coronation of Alexander II, Russian politics were moving toward liberty. He also mentioned the Karakozov Affair, an unsuccessful attempt to murder Alexander II. He must have heard about the affair from Yamauchi Sakuzaemon, supervisor of Japanese students sent by the shogunate to St. Petersburg. Both Mori and Yamauchi agreed that Japan should put an end to her civil war and unite for the purpose of her defense against the Great Powers. Incidentally, Mori had been sent to England by the Satsuma Clan, the greatest rival of the Tokugawa shogunate; so two samurai of opposite camps were in agreement upon their understanding of the situation of the world.

As for Russian foreign policy, Mori wrote of Russia's recent acquisition of the Amur area and the plan to construct railroads from European Russia to Siberia. In this connection, he declared that Russia's final aim was to conquer the whole world, and he warned against the possibility of her invasion of Ezo (Sakhalin and Hokkaido). Emphasizing the necessity of Japanese defense, he pointed out the tremendous size of the Russian land and the huge number of

---

10 Ibid., pp. 73-105

men in her army, which made it difficult for her enemies to gain the final victory. However, he depicted the Russian defeat in the Crimean War as a token of her weakness in spite of the common Japanese view on Russia as a great power.

Against the Japanese evaluation of Russia as a country of justice, Mori ascribed the motivation for the Russian push toward the East to her historical urge to the sea, her desire to obtain ice-free ports. He also mentioned the Russian advance to Sakhalin and her short occupation of Tsushima in 1861 as a proof of her ambition.

In Mori's view on Russia, we can trace the influence of the British press and the views of his tutor, Laurence Oliphant, ex-first secretary of the British legation at Edo (Tokyo) and member of the British Parliament at that time. Oliphant was accustomed to emphasize the Russian menace to Japan out of his experience as a journalist and diplomat.

We should pay special attention to Mori's sharp criticism to the demoralization of Russian society. He noticed two bad features in Russia: one was the disputes among family members for the inheritance, and the other adultery and the birth of children to unmarried girls. However, he admitted that such things were seen not only in Russia but in Japan as well. He was sorry he could not find the final solution to these problems. When we think that he was only nineteen years old at that time, we have to admire his precociousness.

It would be incorrect to say, however, that Mori was pro-Britain and pro-American, and a Russophobe, as is usually said, because a year after his return from Russia, Mori and his four friends sent a long letter to Ōkubo Toshimichi, one of the leaders of the Meiji government and Vice-Ambassador of the Iwakura Mission, emphasizing the aggressive intention of the Great Powers, including Great Britain and the United States. The point is that those young Japanese students had found the real situation of the world as it was: that the stronger prey upon the weaker, and that Russia was neither a country of justice, nor a first-class country in the economic, military and moral sense. They had formed these opinions after their studies of British works and through their own experiences in Western Europe and Russia.

Nineteen years later Mori was appointed the Minister of Education in the first Japanese Cabinet and made every endeavor to establish modern educational systems. He attached special importance to primary education and because of that he gave serious consideration to the normal school. Able and ambitious boys from poor origins were admitted to study in the normal schools without tuition, and teachers were respected everywhere in Japan. The Meiji government issued a law on general education as early as 1872, according to which four years of primary education were declared compulsory. Almost all leaders of the new regime unanimously admitted the importance and the role of education for the modernization of the country, which was not always recognized by the Russian leaders.

It seems to me that for the modernization of a country, in addition to natural resources and to the international environment, success or failure depends upon how well the government attracts and absorbs the energy and ability of the young people. In this sense, the leaders of the Meiji government had the profound insight to set up many institutions for youth with latent ability: army and navy, police, communications, transportation, education, and so forth.[11] They might have become an anti-regime force and appealed to violence.

Needless to say, the Japanese government did not succeed one hundred percent; there was a Movement for Liberty and People's Rights (Jiyū-minken undō) in the 1870's and 1880's which demanded a democratic constitutional regime. But the government repressed the movement without much difficulty and adopted some of their rival's demands as its own program; it issued a Constitution in 1889, 17 years earlier than Russia. What I wish to say is that the Meiji government succeeded comparatively well in recruiting unsatisfied youth to its side, a remarkable contrast with the Russian government, which was unable to establish a general education system until the fall of the monarchy.

*

In juxtaposition with Mori's views, I would like to mention briefly Fukuzawa Yukichi's(1835-1901) views on Russia. Fukuzawa was one of the most brilliant leaders of the enlightenment movement in the early Meiji period. Today, his portrait is used as the design on the Japanese ten thousand yen bill; and every Japanese boy and girl knows that he was a founder of Keio University, one of the most popular private universities in Japan.

Five years before Mori's visit to Russia, Fukuzawa spent about forty days in St. Petersburg as a member of the Takenouchi Embassy. The aim of the Embassy was to negotiate with the Russian government about the frontier problem on Sakhalin and also to postpone the opening of some ports and cities. They succeeded in the latter but not in the former objective. In his autobiography, Fukuzawa wrote that he was astonished to be offered a post in the Russian government by someone in the Russian delegation. Although he had been to the United States and some West Europan countries, he had never been offered a

---

11 Toriyama Shigeto & Togawa Tsuguo *Kindai-ka o meguru hokoku to toron* (Reports and Discussions Concerning Modernization), Slavic Studies, No. 10, Hokkaido University, 1966, pp. 71-84.

post like in Russia, he also found the Russian customs and manners were different from others.[12]

After the Restoration, Fukuzawa told more about Russia in his famous essay Minjō Isshin (Innovation of the People's Mind), published in 1879[13]. In this work he introduced to Japanese readers, perhaps, for the first time, the recent situations in Russia: the autocracy of Nicholas I, the emancipation of serfs by Alexander II, the polemics between Herzen and Katkov, the Karakozov Affair, the nihilists, and so forth. His point was that the more a country civilizes, the more active the anti-governmental movement becomes, and in a country like Russia even an attempt to assasinate the Tsar occurs. On the other hand, in England, where the Parliamentary and two party systems were established, an antagonism such as that in Russia does not exist. Therefore, it is necessary for Japan to adopt the British political systems.

For Fukuzawa, it was obvious that Great Britain was a model and Russia was an anti-model for Japan. Then, from where did he get information about Russia? In order to write about Russian affairs he used Julius Eckardt's Modern Russia Comprising Russia under Alexader II, Russian Communism, The Greek Orthodox Church and Its Sects, The Baltic Provinces of Russia, published in London in 1870. Eckardt was born in Livonia in 1836, and because of his strong anti-Russification sentiment he left Russia to live in Germany and made a career in journalism and politics. Therefore, we can see the influences of his Russo - phobia upon Fukuzawa. In later years Fukuzawa, an ardent westernizer and promoter of "fukoku kyōhei" (enrich the nation and strengthen the army), was to propagandize "datsu-a nyu-ō" (leave Asia and enter Europe) and became a forerunner of the policy of the Japanese invasion of Asia.

*

Five years after the Restoration, the Meiji government sent a special embassy headed by Iwakura Tomomi to fifteen Western countries including Russia.[14] The aim of the Iwakura Mission was not only to prepare the way for revision of the "unequal treaties" concluded by the Tokugawa shogunate, but also to study the Western world for the further advancement of reforms designed

---

12 Fukuzawa Y u k i c h i, *Fukuo Jiden* (The Old Fukuzawa's Autobiography), Iwanami Bunko.

13 Togawa T s u g u o, *Fukuzawa Yukichi to roshia* (Fukuzawa Yukichi and Russia), Mado (Window), Nauka, No. 55, December, 1985, p. 1.

14 Togawa T s u g u o, *Iwakura shisetsu-dan to roshia,* (note no. 4 above).

by the new regime. In this sense, this embassy could be compared to the Grand Embassy of Peter the Great, although the size was smaller (about fifty members and sixty students).

Among the members was a scholar named Kume Kunitake (1839-1931), who compiled a record of the journey and acted as secretary to the Chief Ambassador at the same time. In 1878, he published the record of his journey with the title of Bei-ō Kairan Jikki (A True Account of the Tour in America and Europe). From this record we know that the stay of the Iwakura Mission in the Russian Empire was only for 16 days; from March 30th to April 14th, 1873. This was shorter by far than its stay in the United States for 205 days, in England for 122 days, in France for more than two months, in Germany for about a month. We can also make such a comparison according to the number of chapters ("volumes" in his original record) devoted to individual countries in this record. While Kume included 20 chapters on the United States, and another 20 chapters on England, he wrote only five chapters on Russia. But what he described of this country provides us with interesting images of what the Japanese leaders thought about Russia and the world as well.

They entered Russia after their visits to the United States and West European countries. On the train from Berlin, they saw the ugly sights of poor villages in the season of the thaw. They noticed that the customs inspection at the frontier was more severe than elsewhere, and that the train began to rock after crossing the border. But the splendid scenery of the capital, with huge buildings and palaces, astonished them very much. After having an audience with Emperor Alexander II, they visited a lot of institutions, factories, museums, shipyards and so forth, as they had done in other countries.

When they visited Russia, the country was in the process of the Great Reforms. Although Kume mentioned about the emancipation of the serfs and the improvement of trade, he did not understand correctly the meaning of the reforms. Tanaka Fujimaro, in charge of the section on education, had visited St. Petersburg before the arrival of the Mission, but payed little attention to the educational policy of the Russian government, although he paid much attention to the Prussian educational systems. It is only Ōkubo Toshimichi (1830-78), Vice-Ambassador and head of the Department of Finance, who thought that such countries as England and France were too advanced for Japan to study, and that Prussian and Russian examples would be more helpful to Japanese reforms. He asked Nishi Tokujirō to do special research on financial and internal reforms.

But Ōkubo had to come back home from Berlin before visiting Russia because of an order from Tokyo. We know nothing about whether or not he utilized the results of Nishi's research for setting up the Department of the Interior.

But except for Ōkubo, members of the Iwakura Mission did not seem to find out anything useful in Russia. On the contrary,they regarded the absolute monarchy, the great gap between the rich and the poor, and the illiteracy of the people as a token of the backwardness of the country. In the concluding chapter, Kume wrote that there were five big powers in Europe — England, France, Germany, Austria, and Russia — and that there was a kind of a balance of power among them.

However, Kume says,England and France were the strongest and Russia was the least civilized, and Europeans looked upon her as a country a little superior to Turkey. Japanese people, he continues, have been afraid of Russia since the arrival of the Russian envoy, Nicholai Rezanov, at the outset of the century. But such an image of Russia was nothing but an illusion. It is time for Japan to abandon such a delusion and try to find a country or countries with whom Japan should tie up.

Looking back from the present standpoint, we know that Japan would search for allied nations for decades in a political environment which would become more and more imperialistic, and that she found Great Britain as her cooperator, concluded the Anglo-Japanese Alliance in 1902, and finally declared war against Russia in 1904.

*

Two years after the visit to Russia of the Iwakura Mission, Japan and Russia concluded the Treaty of St. Petersburg by which Japan ceded her common right of territory over Sakhalin to Russia in exchange for the entire Kurile Islands north of Urup. The Treaty gained a very bad reputation in both countries.

Hasegawa Tatsunosuke (1864-1909), who is better known by his pen name of Futabatei Shimei, celebrated translator of Russian novels and founder of the modern Japanese literay style, made up his mind to study Russian immediately after the conclusion of the Treaty. He thought that one day Japan would have to fight with Russia. Therefore, the study of the language of the future enemy would help the fatherland from the peril.

However, while he was studying the Russian language, he became more and more interesed in Russian literature and social thought, such as Gogol's, Turgenev's, Gocharov's, Dostoevsky's, Belinsky's, Herzen's, Dobroliubov's, and so forth. He became doubtful of his former chauvinism and was led, according to his own expression, to the idea of "brotherhood of the world".[15]

Different from most Japanese intellectuals, Futabatei obtained information about Russia from original Russian sources. Before the outbreak of the war, he believed that it was inevitable for both Japan and Russia to have a war, but it was necessary as well not to have a second war. Then he resigned from the post of professor of The Tokyo Institute of Foreign Languages and went to St. Petersburg as correspondent of the Asahi Press. He was sure that both the Japanese and the Russian peoples were against the war, and that the best way to avoid it was for the people to disobey the will of the government to begin the war. For the Japanese and Russian peoples, he thought, the most important thing was to communicate with each other. That was the reason why he went to the Russian capital in 1908. But there he caught tuberculosis and died on his way back home in the following year.

*

In the final part of my report, I would like to mention the doubt of the famous writer Natsume Kinnosuke (1867-1916), who is also better known by his pen name of Natsume Sōseki. You see his portrait on the one thousand yen bill, too. He was not a specialist of Russian literature, but a lecturer in English literature at Tokyo University. In his boyhood, he studied Chinese classics as most Japanese boys did at that time. He was sent to London to study English literature by the government, but he resigned from the post in 1907 and became a free writer and essayist. He is regarded as one of the most popular writers because of his smart and witty style, but his main theme was the antagonism between "ego and society", and most of his heroes were superfluous men like those of Futabatei's and those of the 19th century Russian novels.

In August 1911, Natsume Sōseki delivered a lecture on "The Enlightenment of Contemporary Japan". In this lecture he classified enlightenment into two categories: a voluntary one, the enlightenment from within; and an enforced one, the enlightenment from outside. The European enlightenment, he says, belongs to the former, and the Japanese enlightenment to the latter. He did not say that the former was better and the latter was worse; but he pointed out that the only real, authentic enlightenment was the former. Since peoples in the latter category import enlightenment from abroad, they are always running after the

---

15 Togawa T s u g u o, *Vzgliad iapontsuv na Rossiu: tochka zrenia Utimura Kanzo*, Latyshev, tam zhe, pp. 63-64.

newest things and leave nothing behind them. We Japanese, he says, have the feeling that we are something of hangers-on, and as soon as we get new things we have to abandon them. We always feel in our minds something empty and vain, and we are always unsatisfied and uneasy.[16]

In a word, the enlightenment of contemporary Japan, according to Natsume Sōseki, is false, superficial and frivolous. It is impossible for us to achieve within a decade what the Western nations have done for a century. This is a misery of modern Japan, but we have to accept is as it is. In this way, Natsume Sōseki threw doubts on the essence of the Japanese enlightenment.

It is the late Professor Yamamoto Shin who first pointed out the similar ways of thinking between Natsume Soseki and Peter Chaadaev.[17] Needless to say, Chaadaev also cast doubts on the authenticity of Russian civilization in relation with Western civilization in his famous Philosophical Letters.[18] He depicts the misery of the Russian culture, "a culture based wholly on borrowing and imitation".

Professor Yamamoto, a student of Arnold Toynbee's theory of history, discussed such a similarity of two thinkers from the viewpoint of the relation between the central civilization and the peripheral civilizations. But it seems to me we could approach this problem from the viewpoint of the modernization of late comers as I said at the very beginning of this report.

Unlike Chaadaev, Sōseki did not write "Apology of a Madman", in which Chaadaev stressed the superiority of late comers beause of the possibility of their studying forerunners' experiences. Sōseki remained doubtful until his last days and produced a series of novels which had great influence upon the Japanese intelligentsia. His main theme was, as I have just mentioned, the relation between the modern ego and traditional society, and the establishment of inner, personal liberty within a Japanese life in the process of transformation.

We know that in Russia Alexander Herzen created Russian Socialism, which was based upon three ideas. First, the Western society is old, declining

---

16 Natsume S o s e k i, *Gendai nihon no kaika* (The Enlightenment of Contemporary Japan), Miyoshi Yukio ed., Soseki bunmei-ron shu (Soseki's Essays on Civilization), Iwanami Bunko, 1986, pp. 7-38, esp., pp. 33-35.

17 Yamamoto S h i n, *Soseki to Chaadaev* (Soseki and Chaadaev), Sobun, No. 12, 1973, *Shuhen bunmei toshiteno nihon bunmei to roshia bunmei* (Japanese Civilization and Russian Civilization as Peripheral Civilizations), *Jinbungaku Kenkyujo ho* (Bulletin of the Institite of Humanities), No. 6. Kanagawa University, 1972 and other essays.

18 Chaadaev's Philosophical Letters were translated into Japanese and published with comments by Togawa T s u g u o. *Slavic Studies,* Nos. 6-9, 1962-65.

and comtaminated by "meshchanstvo"; on the other hand Russia is still young, with hopes in the future. Second, Russia could transform into a socialist society on the basis of her traditional peasant communes. Third, it is necessary to introduce individual liberty into the future socialist society, otherwise it would be an autocratic society with communism upside down. Here we can see the same idea of the superiority of late comers as was the case with Peter Chaadaev.[19]

In Japan, there were also such people as Itagaki Taisuke (1837-1919), a distinguished leader of the Movement for Liberty and People's Rights and a nationalist convert after his visit to Europe, who depicted the corruption and so forth. He was much impressed by the colonialism of Western powers in the East, which he noticed on his way to and back from Europe. Such observations caused him to become more nationalistic and brought him close to the Establishment.

*

At present, not only Western journalists but also Soviet scholars admit the success of the modernization of Japan[20], and they have especially high regard for Japanese achievements in technology. Among them, some people even admire the harmony between Japan's traditional way of life and the modern Western lifestyle. In this sense, the slogan of "tōyō dōtoku, seiyō geijutsu' (the East is superior in morals, the West is superior in science) was marvelously realized in Japan. But the fact is not so simple as it looks in appearance or in statistics, since the essence of modernization exists not in a change of life-style but in a change in the way of thinking or value systems. In this connection, the second modernizing process of Japan began with her defeat in World War II. Like the first one, the Meiji Restoration, this second start was also made by the impact from outside, i.e. the U.S. occupation and reforms after the end of the War.

As to the Japanese view on the Soviet Union, there are two factors which have had a dominant influence upon the the nation. One is the experience of about six hundred thousand war prisoners. Most of them were taken from Manchuria and Sakhalin to Siberia after the War. Another is the American view on the Soviet Union. But this is not the place to discuss this question, which is beyond the scope of my report.

---

19 cf. Togawa T s u g u o, *Gerutsen to roshia shakai* (Herzen and the Russian Society) Ochanomizu Press, Tokyo, 1973.

20 For example in his lecture entitled *Problems of the Comparative Historical Analysis of Modernization* delivered at Sophia University, May 10th, 1989, Dr. Vladimir K h o r o s of the Institute of International Economics and International Relations highly evaluated Japanese achievements.

Wasilij Szczukin — Université Jagellonne, Cracovie.

Vissarion Biélinski et sa rencontre avec l'Occident

Le 5/17/ mai 1847 un célébre critique littéraire Vissarion Biélinski quitta Pétersbourg et se rendit à l'étranger. Il passa deux mois et demi en Allemagne faisant sa cure à la station thérmale à Salzbrunn et visitant Berlin, Dresde, la Suisse Saxe, la Silésie-Inférieure, Frankfourt et Cologne.Ensuite il traversa la Balgique et atteignit Paris. Pavel Anniénkov et Ivan Tourguéniev, deux hommes de lettres, camarades de Biélinski, l'accompagnaient presque pendant tout son voyage, tandis qu'en France le critique non seulement demeurait à la maison de santé à Passy, mais tenait aussi la companie à Alexandre Herzen qui ne devint encore un émigré politique, de même qu'à Mikhaïl Bakounine et Nikolaï Sazonov qui représentaient l'émigration.

C'est depuis longtemps que Biélinski aspirant à se mettre en voyage étranger et qu'il enviait ses amis dont l'aisance permettait de partir pour Paris, Berlin ou Rome.[1] Etant gravement malade, sans argent (son voyage étranger fut financé grâce aux bienfaits des amis) il rêvait de l'Occident comme du pays de Cocagne. "Peut-être il y aura une possibilité de jeter un coup d'oeil de la porte du paradis"[2], écrit-il à Vassili Botkine le 17/29 février 1847.

Quelle était donc sa rencontre avec l'Occident? Il y a deux versions à ce sujet-là. Selon la première, celle de Tourguéniev et d'Anniénkov qui observaient le comportement de Biélinski à l'étranger de leurs propres yeux, le critique fut déçu, parce que la réalité européenne ne correspondait pas à ses imaginations. Les mémoires écrits par ses deux compagnons referment des détails intéressants qui illustrent cette attitude de Biélinski envers le réel Occident, l'attitude semblant tout à fait étrange, si l'on veut parler de l'homme adorant tout ce qu'était occidental. Or, Biélinski semblait indifférent à tout ce qui concernait les curiosités historiques, artistiques et culturelles: il ne voulait pas visiter la

---

1 Voir les lettres de Biélinski à V. Botkine datées du 22 novembre 1839 et du 22 février 1840, in V. G. B i é l i n s k i, *Polnoïé sobraniïé sotchiniénii, vol. 11, Editions d'Etat des Belles Lettres,* Moscou, 1956, p. 420, 464, et surtout la lettre à P. Kudriavtsev datée du 28 novembre 1841, ibidem, vol. 12, p. 57.

2 Ibidem, vol. 12, p. 329.

cathédrale de Cologne, il ne parlait que de Gogol sur la place de la Concorde et il n'a pas trouvé la Madone Sixtine de Rafael trop aristocratique, trop méprisante "à l'égard de nous qui sommes des racailles".[3] En même temps il s'émerveillait de la doucer de la nature et de la splendeur de la civilisation matérielle; il admirait surtout des beaux magasins de Paris.[4] Les lettres confirment cette version-là. Des motifs du mécontement, des plaintes, des persiflages même se trouvent sur les pages de ces documents témoignants des difficultés qui découlaient de la confrontation avec l'Occident. En Silésie c'était la libérté qui lui manquait toujours, puisq'il ne pouvait pas faire des promenades n'importe où,là où il voudrait: il n'y avait pas de terrains sans propriétaire comme en Russie, des gens étrangers qui vivaient à l'étroit le gênaient partout...[5]. Le capitalisme primitif avec son paupérisme et avec sa platitude de la bourgeoise triomphante ne lui plaisaient point; il haïssait ardemment la modération, le bon sens et la prudence des Allemands ?"Ils ont pas le sang, mais la mauvaise bière dans leurs fibres"?[7], il raillissait l'Eglise catholique. En même temps, au cours de sa fameuse discussion au sujet du capitailsme entre Herzen, Bakounine, Sazonov et les libéraux (comme Botkine et Anniénkov) Biélinski n'était pas tout à fait d'accord avec le point dès vue de Herzen qui croyait que la bourgeoisie était inhumaine et réactionnaire dè le moment de sa naissance et que le capitalisme c'était la maladie mortelle du monde romano-germain, par excellence féodal. Anniénkov, et surtout Tourguéniev epliquaient le désintéressement ou le désappointement de Biélinski tout simlement: il était gravement malade, n'avait plus de sa vitalité, il n'était pas suffisamment prêt à percevoir culture occidentale. Et enfin, ajoutaient-ils, une pareille réaction psychique est un trait accentué de chaque voyageur russe qui se trouve pour la première fois en Europe[7].

---

3 Voir ibidem, vol. 12, p. 284 (la lettre à V.Botkine datée du 7/19 juillet 1847), de même que P. V. A n n i é n k o v, *Litiératurnyïe vospominanïïa, Editions d'Etat des Belles Lettres,* Moscou, 1960, p. 351, 363, 365-369 et I. S. T o u r g u é n i e v, *Polnoïé sobranïïé sotchiniénïï i pisiem v 28 tomakh: Sotchiniénïïa v 15 tomakh,* vol. 14, Editions d'Académie des Sciences de l'URSS, Moscou - Léningrad, 1967, p. 54 - 55.

4 Voir P.V. A n n i é n k o v, op. cit., p. 371 - 372; V.G. B i é l i n s k i, op. cit., vol. 12, p. 387 (la lettre à V. Botkine datée du 22 juillet/3 août 1847).

5 Voir la lettre écrite par Biélinski à sa femme datée du 24 mai/5 juin 1847, in V.G. B i é l i n s k i, op. cit., vol. 12, p. 367 -368.

6 Ibidem, vol. 12, p. 383 (la lettre à V. Botkine datée du 7/19 juillet 1847).

7 Botkine écrivit dans sa lettre à P. Anniénkov datée du 20 mars 1847; "Quiconque de nous venant en Europe commence à raisonner sur le sujet d'elle par des niaiseries!" (*Anniénkov i ïego drouzïa. Litiératournyïe vospominanïïa i piériépiska 1835 -1885 godov.* Saint-Pétersbourg, 1892, p. 533).

Par ailleurs quelques savants soviétiques, se croyant marxistes, tels que D. Zaslavski et V. Nietchaïeva, proposent une autre version. Selon eux la désapprobation de l'Occident que fut manifestée par Biélinski peut être interpretée comme une expression de la mentalité toute proche de celle de Marx et d'Engels. Les partisants de cette version affirment que le critique russe repoussa le libéralisme avec son apologie du capitalisme autant que le socialisme utopique, chrétien ou anarchiste représenté par P. Le Roux, L. Blanc, F. Lamennais et M. Bakounine.[8] Pourtant cette argumentation ne prend pas en considération ce que Biélinski critiquait certaines doctrines sociales et politiques en ne faisant aucune expérience de la vie authentique de l'Europe. L'image de l'Occident qui s'était formée dans sa conscience n'était basée que sur l'imagination d'après la littérature. A cause de cela on ne peut pas comparer la pensée de Biélinski avec celle des penseurs occidentaux. Et alors, après son retour à Pétersbourg il devint plus "opportuniste" et moins "anticapitaliste" qu'autrefois.

En effet, les définitions comme "socialiste", "libéral", "idéologue de capitalisme" etc. considerées au sens occidental de ces termes ne conviennent pas aux intellectuels russes des années quarante du XIX-138me siècle, puisque le rôle principal de ces hommes consistait en civilisation générale de sa société et en propagation de l'éducation moderne et pas justement "bourgeoise" ou "socialiste". On peut aussi affirmer que sa désapprobation des éléments essentiels de la civilisation romano-germaine, notamment le bon sens, l'exactitude ou bien la prudence, fut un élan cordial de Biélinski et pas un fruit de ses études économiques et sociologiques.

Je crois qu'il faut considérer la confrontation de Biélinski avec l'Occident dans le contexte socio-psychologique de son individualité.

Le chemin qui menait Biélinski à Paris était long. Il passa l'enfance et l'adolescence à Tchémbar, une petite ville, presqu'un village, située dans la région de Pénza, près de 600 km au sud-est de Moscou. C'était un vrai coin perdu dans lequel la grande majorité des habitants formait la paysannerie; il n'y avait là qu'une rue bordée de bastides et qu'une place centrale qui se présentait comme une pelouse.[9] Jeune Biélinski, très ambitieux et doué, croissait dans le

8 D.O. Zaslavski, *K voprosou o polititchéskom zaviéchtchanii Biélinskogo,* in Litiératournoïe naslédstvo, vol. 55, Editions d'Académie des Sciences de l'URSS, Moscou, 1948, p. 51 - 86; V.S. Niétchaïeva, V.G. Biélinski: *Zhizn i tvortchestvo, 1842 - 1848,* Editions d'Académie des Sciences de l'URSS, Moscou, 1967, p. 321 -383.

9 Voir V.S. Niétchaïeva, V.G. Biélinski: *Natchalo zhizniénnogo pouti i litiératournoï diéiatiélnosti, 1811 - 1830,* Editions d'Academie des Sciences de l'URSS, Moscou, 1949, p. 50 - 54.

millieu de la médiocratie provinciale, parmi des fonctionnaires et des prêtres illettrés. Un petit homme de talent condamné à l'existence désespérée et provinciale, à quoi rêvait-il? Il regarde toujours du côté du foyer de la civilisation, il désire y aller, il veut être digne de vivre parmi les gens élevés et culturels. Tel était le complexe de province et de "plébéisme" que Biélinski possédait sans doute.

Il commence à étudier. Cependant au gymnase de Pénza il manque les leçons de français, car il ne connaissait pas du tout cette langue, tandis que des autres élèves parlaient français avec leurs parents et n'avaient aucune difficulté à l'utiliser.[10] Il veut pourtant entrer à l'Université de Moscou, et pour passer l'examen d'entrée il doit connaître bien le français; à cause de cela il prend les leçons chez un répétiteur. Il arrive enfin à Moscou, il devient étudiant à l'université. Mais... il se trouva qu'il y avait sur la terre d'autres centres de culture et de progrès: Berlin avec ses écoles philosophiques, Paris avec ses mouvements politiques. Biélinski était loin du cosmopolitisme, mais il possédait toujours la connaissance de la nécessité de ne pas être en arrière de l'avant-garde du monde.

C'etait la connaissance typique pour chacun qui était venu de la province et qui était pris pour un parvenu mal élevé dans le milieu aristocratigue. Après dix ans de séjour Moscou lui semble déjà provinciale; son esprit de civilisateur (allem. *Kulturträger*, russe *prosviétitiel*) l'oblige à rompre les liasons avec le cercle philosophique où regnait le culte de l'esprit absolu et dont le climat devenait de plus en plus étouffant pour quelqu'un qui avait décidé de prendre part au mouvement progressif du genre humain — non seulement comme un contemplateur, mais comme un participant actif. Le désir d'être au milieu de la vie littéraire (aussi bien que l'espoir de gagner davantage) l'amena à Pétersbourg qui était"la fenêtre par laquelle la Russie regardait en Europe"[11], et à cause de cela on y prenait la vie à la manière occidentale (notamment le pragmatisme, l'équilibre, le bon sens) pour une chose naturelle.

A partir de 1841 Biélinski se mit à la tête de l'occidentalisme. Les adeptes de ce courant mental tentaient d'appliquer la philosophie d'action empruntée à la gauche du hégélianisme à la réalité russe, en attaquant les slavophiles, partisants du conservatisme romantique. Les occidentalistes considéraient l'occident sous deux aspects. Selon le premier point de vue c'était l'Europe

---

[10] Voir ibidem, p. 185 - 186.

[11] La célèbre maxime mise par Francesco Algarotti (1712 - 1764), écrivain et savant italien, dans son livre intitulé *Lettres sur la Russie* (1739). Cette métaphore fut utilisée par Alexandre Pouchkine dans son poème Le Cavalier de Bronze.

Occidentale avec ses propres problèmes. Dans ce monde-là, croyait-on, le républicanisme luttait contre des détritus du monarchisme, des germes du socialisme — contre le libéralisme etc. Le deuxième aspect c'était l'Occident considéré en bloc, comme un idéal auquel la Russie doit aspirer. A ce dernier point de vue le féodalisme, la monarchie et aussi le capitalisme devaient être considérés comme progressistes par raport à l'autocratie patriarcale et à l'arriération de la Russie.

Biélinski se passionnait de Robespierre et de "la sainte Guillotine" (à partir de 1841 et jusqu'à 1845, mais pas plus tard), il prenait intérêt au socialisme de Fourier et de Louis Blanc ou même d'Engels (avant 1847) en tant qu'un homme marchant au pas avec son époque. Cependant ce n'était pas tout cela qu'il cherchait à l'Occident pour accomplir la mission principale de sa vie — s'approcher avec sa patrie du vrai Centre de la Civilisation, mettre fin au provincialisme russe. C'est pourquoi il adorait spontanément tous les indices de la prospérité et du comfort: chemins de fer, confiseries, restaurants[12] — et non seulement les monuments historiques ou les chefs-d'oeuvre artistiques. Pour se distinguer des penseurs romantiques (par exemple Bakounine) Biélinski savait bien que sa patrie a besoin de la civillisation générale et non seulement des idées européennes qui étaient considérées comme "progressistes".

Le problème de la place de la Russie dans la civilisation générale occupait tojours Biélinski et se développait graduellement. Au début des années quarante sa devise principale était formulée de la manière suivante: la Russie ce n'est pas l'Asie, elle appartient à l'Europe, royaume du progrès humain.[13] L'appartenance à L'Europe signifiait naturellement que la Russie était la province éloignée de ce royaume. Les Russes n'ont créé rien de considérable pour le moment; leur mentalité, leurs problèmes et leur littérature n'étaient pas des chosse qui pourraient intéresser l'Occident. Cette conception fut subitement ébranlée en 1845, quand Biélinski apprit que les oeuvres de Gogol traduites par Paul Viardot avaient eu du grand succès en France, et en 1846, quand un jeune critique Valérian Maïkov dèclara qu'il fallait abandonner des positions d'originalité nationale comme un préjugé réactionnaire. Biélinski blâma Maîkov dans son article *Un coup d'oeil sur littérature russe en 1846*. Il considéra le problème de la nationalité en y appliquant la méthode dialectique. "Il est temps de cesser d'admirer l'Europe uniquement parce qu'elle n'est pas l'Asie, écrivit-il, — il est nécessaire de l'aimer, de l'estimer, d'aspirer à l'Occident

---

[12] Voir par exemple la lettre de Biélinski à sa femme datée du 24 juin 1846, in V. G. B i é l i n s k i, op. cit., vol. 12, p. 292.

[13] Ibidem, vol. 5, p. 98, 105, 132, 144 -145 (l'article intitulé *La Russie avant Pierre le Grand*).

parce que c'est l'esprit human qui demeure là".[14] Et l'esprit humain, ajoutait-il, n'est pas quelque chose d'abstrait, il ne se manifeste que dans des nations. C'est pourquoi il faut considérer l'esprit national, la mentalité originale de certaine nation comme un phénomène positif. Tout cela concerne aussi les Russes.

Mais comment sont les Russes? Est-ce qu'ils ont créé certaines valeurs qui pourraient être introduites dans la culture universelle? Biélinski pensait beaucoup à ce sujet; il avait plusiers doutes à cet égard—- et voilà ce qu'il écrivit deux mois avant son départ à l'étranger, impressionné après la lecture du roman *Bataille de la vie* de Dickens:

Je respecte les hommes pratiques — mais pas au prix de l'esprit borné, de l'étroitesse étouffante comme celle de ce stupide Anglais! Il est mieux d'être contemplateur, mais ressentir tout de façon large, juste et profonde. Je suis Russe d'après nature. Et je suis fier d'être Russe. Je ne veux pas être même un Français. L'individu russe est un embryon pour ce moment, mais que d'ampleur et de vigueur renferme la nature de cet embryon, pour qui chaque étroitesse est si étouffante! (...) Et alors, peut-être il me semble que nous embrassons le monde entier parce que nous n'avons rien à faire? Non, à mesure que je pense davantage à ce sujet, je m'en assure moi-même que c'est un mensonge. Les Géorgiens n'ont rien à faire non plus — mais entre eux il n'y a pas du tout des individus remarquables. Le Russe est un zéro, mais il est exigeant: il ne veut pas de ceci, il demande cela, il aspire à quelque chose....[15]

Telles étaient les opinions de Biélinski la veille de son voyage en Europe. Il n'est pas étonnant qu'il se sent étranger au monde romano-germain, avec son aménagement qui ne put être atteint que grâce à "l'étroitesse" de l'espace et de l'esprit européen . L'Occident réel satisfaisait les pires pressentiments du critique. A Paris il savait bien qu'il ne pouvait pas devenir un émigré et habiter toujours dans ce "centre du monde civilisé — la proposition d'émigration présentée par Bakounine fut rejetée résolument".

Quelques-uns des occidentalistes craignaient que Biélinski commence la bataille contre le capitalisme et qu'il grossisse les rangs des adversaires de l"occident "pourri".[16] Eh bien, la tentation était forte: par exemple, Herzen n'a pas pu y résister. A tout propos dès son retour en Russie Biélinski intensifia ses attaques contre les slavophiles, évolua vers les valeurs libérales et accepta même le capitalisme comme l'unique forme possible du développement futur de sa

---

[14] Ibidem, vol. 10, p. 19.

[15] Ibidem, vol. 12, p. 350 (la lettre à V.Botkine datée du 8 mars 1847).

[16] Voir P.V. A n n i é n k o v, op. cit., p. 310.

patrie, quoiqu'il ne dissimule pas sa désaffection à propos du progrès à la manière bourgeoise. Des idéaux d'occidentalisme russe, de la civilisation générale de la Russie s'avérèrent pour lui plus importants que des engouements populistes.[17]

Pourquoi cela s'est passé ainsi? On peut confirmer qu'il y avait deux raisons principales pour lesquelles Biélinski ne devint pas un ennemi de l'Occident, comme Bakounine, Herzen et beaucoup d'autres intellectuels russes.

La première raison est facile à comprendre: en Allemagne et en France Biélinski vécut en dehors de la polémique entre les occidentalistes et les slavophiles -en Russie il s'avèrait que chaque ennemi du capitalisme devenait automatiquement un partisant de l'utopie patriarcale des slavophiles. La logique de la bataille littéraire et idéologique menait Biélinski vers le libéralisme démocratique.

La deuxième raison s'ensuit d'un trait particulier de son crédo philosophique, qui était le réalisme. C'était d'abord le réalisme naïf de l'homme né à Tchémbar, ensuite le réalisme du prolétaire intellectuell et enfin le réalisme du penseur, fruit des réflexions et des souffrances.Les slavophiles étaient traditionnalistes romantiques, élèves de Schelling. Un autre romantisme nourissait le coeur de Herzen, de Bakounine, d'Ogariov et des autres représentants de l'aristoctatie gauche. C'était la poésie de la révolution sociale, y compris la mort du monde actuel et l'édification de "l'harmonie totale". On peut affirmer que toutes les variétés du romantisme (inclusivement l'anticapitalisme) étaient quelque chose d'étrange pour Biélinski. La rébellion contre l'Occident *réel*, selon lui, était sans doute une rébellion contre *la réalité*, contre l'ordre naturel des choses. Le choc que Biélinski avait éprouvé en Allemagne et en France démontra l'incompatibilité de son caractère à ce monde complètment lui étranger. Il se rendait pourtant compte, que tout cela ne concernait que lui-même et non pas toute la Russie, comme l' é t a t qui devait se moderniser. L'apathie qui s'empara de Biélinski étant en Europe, c'était une apathie d'un comtemplateur qui voulait comprendre le secret de la puissance matérielle et spirituelle de ce monde, semblant médiocre. La réalité de l'Occident fut donc justifiée par Biélinski comme une sorte d'indispensabilité historique.

Rappelons-nous comment Biélinski tâchait de s'avancer: en marchant de la province à la capitale, de la périphérie de l'Europe aux centres culturels de cette partie du monde. Tandis que les aristocrates moscovites, comme Herzen et Bakounine, s'imaginaient l'Occident comme un berceau de la révolution

---

[17] Cf. A. W a l i c k i, *W kręgu konserwatywnej utopii: Struktura i przemiany rosyjskiego słowianofilstwa*, Editions Scientifiques d'Etat, Varsovie, 1964, p. 356 - 359.

mondiale, pour Biélinski c'étaient des conquêtes du long processus civilisateur qui l'intéressaient au plus haut degré. Avant son départ à l'étranger il savait bien ce qui était nécessaire pour vaincre l'arriération russe: ce n'était pas le socialisme, c'étaient des fabriques et des banques, des chemins de fer et des chaussées, des institutions républicaines et démocratiques.

Il me semble qu'avant son voyage Biélinski savait bien aussi qu'il ne deviendrait jamais citoyen du monde, c'est à dire *homo occidentalis* (que prétendait devenir, par exemple, Bakounine). Ses lettres, ses articles et les mémoires des contemporains démontrent que c'était la vie russe et pas occidentale qui l'intéressait le plus profondément. C'est pourquoi il ne tâchait pas de prendre en affection la cathédrale de Cologne ou la mentalité des Allemands ou des Français. Cependant son "esprit civilisateur" lui suggérait: cela ne fait rien que le monde romano-germain est étranger pour les Russes. Il y a donc l'unique chemin sur lequel les peuples marchent l'un après l'autre. On peut réprouver les formes concrètes de la vie européenne, mais personne n"est capable de réprouver les lois universelles du progrès.C'est pourquoi la Russie a besoin de l'Occident qui doit être un idéal, un symbole de l'avant-garde de l'humanité.

Il faut remarquer que les intellectuels russes devenaient des vrais *homini occidentali* très rarement (seulement le prince Pierre Kozlovski, le comte Ivan Gagarine, Ivan Tourguéniev et Pavel Anniénkov viennent à l'esprit). La plupart des émigrés russes, en XIX-138me et en XX-138me siècle, maudisaient "l'Occident pourri". Les vrais occidentalistes, ainsi que Biélinski, demeuraient loin de ce royaume symbolique, que paraissait l'Occident dans leur imagination.

Michel Cadot — Université de la Sorbonne Nouvelle, Paris

Un livre injustement oublié: la Russie et l'Europe d'Henri Martin (1866)

Ce livre d'un historien autrefois aussi célèbre que Michelet, mais dont le nom n'évoque plus aujourd'hui qu'une des avenues chic du 16ème arrondissement de Paris, est intéressant à tirer de l'oubli dans la perspective ouverte par ce colloque, et pour plusieurs raisons.

1) Henri Martin s'inscrit dans la tradition de l'historiographie française libérale favorable à la cause polonaise du dix-neuvième siècle.

2) Il continue les attaques de Michelet et de Mickiewicz contre la Russie, mais, plus nettement que ceux-ci, prétend la rejeter vers l'Asie où, selon lui, se situe son avenir aussi bien que son passé.

3) Ce livre est (selon moi) à la base de celui de Danilevski, de même titre, et des dernières pages du *Journal d'un Ecrivain* de Dostoïevski.

Je développerai successivement ces trois points, sans naturellement entrer dans un détail minutieux auquel renverront les notes du texte écrit.

On sait que la «question polonaise» a hanté l'opinion française de 1830 à 1863, c'est-à-dire toute la période qui sépare les deux grands soulèvements polonais du XIXème siècle. Aucun gouvernement, ni celui de Louis-Philippe, ni la Seconde République, ni le Second Empire, pourtant vainqueur de la Russie en 1855, n'a sérieusement voulu la reconstitution d'un Etat polonais. En revanche une partie importante de l'opinion publique française, depuis les catholiques de la tendance Montalembert jusqu'aux républicains comme Barbès ou le Victor Hugo de l'exil, continue de soutenir la cause polonaise dans les revues, les journaux, au Parlement ou dans la rue.

Henri Martin, né en 1810 à Saint-Quentin, jeune provincial romantique,«monte» à Paris en 1830. Historien de tendance libérale, il s'engage dans la vie politique avant et pendant la Révolution de 1848. Défenseur convaincu des nationalités, il publie une série d'articles du 6 février au 24 juin 1863 dans Le Siècle qu'il publie le 15 août sous forme d'une brochure de 63 pages intitulée de façon caractéristique *Pologne et Moscovie*. On y lit par exemple p. 25:

Que les gouvernements aient leurs procédés diplomatiques, leur marche progressive dans le développement des questions de fait, c'est leur affaire et non la nôtre ... L'opinion a, elle, sa marche à part... Pour elle, il n'y a pas le droit contre le droit, point de traités de 1815. Le mouvement actuel dans sa force et sa netteté, ne s'arrête pas, en réagissant contre le mal, à telle ou telle phase du mal: il remonte à la source même: il est la négation de tout ce qui s'est fait depuis 1772.

L'historien Gabriel Hanotaux publie dans son livre de 1885 une longue lettre d'Henri Martin à un ami italien nommé Peruzzi, datée du 16 novembre 1863. Il refuse de condamner la Pologne, comme le faisait Proudhon, qui ne voyait en elle qu'une résurrection de fanatisme catholique et d'oligarchie nobiliaire».[1] Une Pologne ressuscitée ne peut être que multiconfessionnelle et démocratique. Quant à la Russie, «elle manifeste ouvertement sa vraie nature tartare»[2], et Henri Martin prophétise, une fois la France elle-même revenue à la démocratie, un duel à mort «entre le Comité de Salut Public et Gengis-Khan, et Dieu sait tout ce qui serait broyé entre les deux».[3]

Il est intéressant d'observer qu'en cette même année 1863 une polémique assez vive opposait la revue des frères Dostoïevski, Le Temps (Vremja) à la revue conservatrice de Katkov *Le Messager russe* (*Russkij Vestnik*), au sujet de la Pologne. Katkov écrivait dans un article intitulé "La question polonaise" (24 février 1863): «La question de la Pologne a toujours été la question de la Russie. Entre ces deux nationalités issues d'une même tribu l'historie a depuis longtemps posé la question fatale, la question de vie et de mort».[4] Un article signé *Un Russe* parut en écho à celui de Katkov sous le titre "La question fatale" dans *Le Temps* de mai 1863. Il était de N.N. Strakhov, ami de Dostoïevski puis de Tolstoï et alors collaborateur de la revue de Dostoïevski. Celui-ci écrivait à Tourguéniev le 17 juin: «La pensée en était que les Polonais nous ont voué un tel mépris comme à des barbares, tirent un tel orgueil de leur civilisation européenne, qu'une réconciliation morale (c'est-à-dire la plus solide) entre eux et nous est à peu près hors de prévision...».[5] Dans l'article de Strakhov l'asia-

---

1 G. H a n o t a u x, *Henri Martin. Sa vie — ses oeuvers — son temps 1810-1883*, Paris, L. Cerf, 1885, p. 202.

2 Ibid., p. 204.

3 Ibid., p. 206.

4 F. M. D o s t o e v s k i j, *Polnoe sobranie sočinenii v 30 tomax*, t. 20, Léningrad 1980, p. 317.

5 Citée et traduite dans Dostoïevski, *Récits chroniques et polémiques*, éd. G. Aucouturier. Bibl. de la Pléiade, 1969, p. 1811-2, *P. S. S.*, t. 28/2, Léningrad 1985, p. 34.

tisme des Russes était opposé à l'européisme des Polonais: devant les violentes critiques des *Nouvelles de Moscou* (*Moskovskie Vedomosti*), autre revue conservatrice, Dostoïevski prit la défense de son collaborateur, qu'il désigne par son nom, et soutient qu'il n'était question dans tout l'article que du point de vue des Polonais, et non bien entendu de celui de la revue *Le Temps*.[6] Quoi qu'il en soit, la teneur de l'article de Strakhov fut présentée au public français dans la très influente *Revue des Deux Mondes* du ler août 1863 par un ardent défenseur de la cause polonaise, Carles de Mazade, qui l'attribue à... Dostoïevski lui-même. Dans ses *Souvenirs* publiés en 1885, Strakhov écrit: «La revue y trouva confirmation de ses propres vues sur le soulèvement polonais [...] Mazade attribua mon article à Dostoïevski et, à cette occasion, parla de son exil et de ses ouvrages.Il déclare entre autres: *il a écrit des livres navrants sur sa patrie*».[7] L'article de Mazade, on l'imagine aisément, fut connu d'Henri Martin, aussi très occupé de la question polonaise en cette même année 1863. Il allait dans le même sens que la réédition des *Légendes démocratiques du Nord* de Michelet (1854) parue en mars 1863 sous le nouveau titre *La Pologne martyr — Russie — Danube*, avec une nouvelle préface où Michelet déclarait: «La Pologne est le coeur du Nord — *elle seule et non l'autre*, qui est d'Asie, sauf quelques Parisiens de Pétersbourg et d'illustres disciples d'Hégel qui ne changeront pas cette grosse masse où rien ne mord».[8] Ces quelques lignes sont citées par Henri Martin dans les *Eclaircissements* de son livre de 1866.[9]

La Russie et l'Europe parut avec retard, dit Hanotaux[10], à un moment où l'affaire polonaise paraissait définitivement réglée. Comme Michelet avec ses *Légendes*. H. Martin eut le tort de voir trop loin dans l'avenir et de se montrer aveugle en face de la menace allamande imminente: les générations françaises qui suivirent, traumatisées par trois guerres successives contre l'allemagne, minimsèrent à leur tour le danger mondial que représenta la révolution russe sous sa forme stalino-brejnévienne. Henri Martin inscrit en épigraphe de son livre une application particulière de la doctrine de Monroe: «L'Europe aux Européens». Toute sa thèse consiste à soutenir que la Russie est par essence étrangère à l'Europe:

> L'Europe est une association point ou mal réglée, une diversité de nations qui n'a encore de son harmonie qu'une conscience imparfaite.

---

6 D o s t o e v s k i j, *P. S. S.*, t. 20, p. 97-101.
7 Ibid., p. 318.
8 J. M i c h e l e t, Légendes démocratiques du Nord, éd. M. Cadot, P. U. F., 1968, p. 7.
9 H. M a r t i n, La Russie et l'Europe, Paris, Furne, 1866, p. 411.
10 G. H a n o t a u x, op. cit., p. 206.

La Russie est une unité qui prend conscience d'elle-même dans le despotisme par lequel et pour lequel elle est constituée.[11]

Certes on peut sourir de la théorie «touranienne» ou tartare qui fait de l'Etat russe l'héritier d'Attila, Gengis-Khan, Timour-Leng et des sultans ottomans. Mickiewicz ne disait pas autre chose dans son cours au Collège de France.[12] Ce qui fait l'originalité du point de vue d'Henri Martin, c'est de réduire la question de Pologne à un épisode de la question russo-européenne, «mais c'est l'épisode central sur lequel pivote tout le reste».[13] Ce qui s'est passé sous nos yeux au XX-138me siècle, depuis l'apparition au début des années quatre-vingt de Solidarność, confirme absolument cette idée, et la contagion démocratique qui en a résulté, des pays Baltes jusqu'à la Bulgarie, place en effet l'Europe devant de nouvelles et immenses responsabilités, où la solidité de l'entente franco-allemande va jouer un rôle déterminant. Que disait Henri Martin dans sa conclusion?

> La lointaine utopie de la Fédération européenne sera une réalité le jour où la France et l'Allemagne seront réconciliées:
>
> «Le jour où l'Allemagne brisera le pacte de ses princes avec l'ENNEMI DE L'EUROPE et donnera les mains à une réaction radicale contre les faits prétendus accomplis en Pologne depuis un siècle... Les faits qui se sont passés en Pologne, depuis 1772, n'ont constitué qu'un désordre croissant: de période en période, l'occupation moscovite en Pologne est devenue une violation plus éclatante des principes de notre civilisation, une perturbation plus profonde de l'Europe, une menace plus prochaine pour la société européenne tout entière...»[14]

Que fait en ce moment même l'Allemagne de l'Est, si n'est se rapprocher d'un seul coup de l'Europe occidentale, et comment mieux qualifier que par les mots même d'Henri Martin le long cauchemar que toute une moitié de l'Europe a vécu et vit encore en partie depuis près de cinquante ans?

---

[11] H. M a r t i n, op. cit., p. I.

[12] Voir mon article *Michelet, Mickiewicz et la Russie...*, dans Messianisme et Slavophilie, Cracovie 1987, p. 45 et 49.

[13] H. M a r t i n, préface, p.III.

[14] H. M a r t i n, p. 308.

Mal composé, le livre d'Henri est par moments illisible, tout encombré de développements historiques ou ethnographiques largement dépassés. Cependant il faut observer que cet historien français connaît et utilise Haxthausen, Schnitzler, Koulich, Pogodine, Herzen, Soloviov et bien entendu le Polonais Franciszek Duchinski, premier inventeur de la théorie touranienne, qui nie l'appartenance des Moscovites à la race aryenne, et par voie de conséquence les oppose aux Slaves.[15] Au passage Henri Martin dénonce le «terrorisme tartare» de 1863-64, «nullemant spontané, mais calculé et froidement systématique», et stigmatise le rôle néfaste de Katkov, infatigable dénonciateur «de tout ce qui en Russie témoigne un sentiment humain».[16]

D'origine asiatique, la Russie, aux yeux d'Henri Martin, doit être détournée de l'Europe à laquelle elle est étrangère, et encouragée à s'installer en Asie. J'ai essayé de montrer lors du VIème Symposium International Dostoevsky à Nottingham (août 1986) qu'on pouvait établir une relation complexe entre *La Russie et l'Europe* d'Henri Martin (1866), *Rossija i Evropa* de Danilevski (1869), et le *Journal d'un Ecrivain* de Dostoïevski pour l'année 1881.[17]

Dans une note en bas des pages 316 et 317 de son livre, comme une espèce de post-scriptum à la conclusion, Henri Martin écrit ces lignes capitales pour notre sujet:

> Les établissements de la Russie, dans l'extrême Orient, offrent aujourd'hui un grand problème. Si les Moscovites n'étaient pas campés au coeur de l'Europe, où ils ne peuvent faire que le mal, nous ne nous inquiéterions pas de les voir créer quelque chose sur le fleuve Amour, où il n'y avait rien, et nous n'entendons pas nier, par exemple, que la communication télégraphique entre les deux hémisphères, à travers les déserts du nord du globe, soit en elle-même un progrès. Un vaste champ d'activités pourrait être là ouvert légitimement aux Moscovites pour appliquer les leçons qu'ils ont reçues de l'Europe et qu'ils tournent contre l'Europe.

---

15 Voir la note au t. 20 de Dostoevskij, P. S. S., p. 383. Son livre s'intitulait en toute simplicité *Peuples Aryas et Tourans agriculteurs et l'historie des peuples aryas-européens et tourans, particulièrement des Slavs et des Moscovites*, 1864, Dostoïevski y fait allusion dans une note du 30 août 1864 (p. 191).

16 H. Martin, op. cit., p. 384.

17 M. Cadot, *Le discours sur le dutur dans le Journal d'un Ecrivain*, 1881, Remarques sur le prophétisme de Dostoïevski, dans Dostoevsky Studies. Journal of the International Dostoevsky Society, vol. 7, 1986, p. 19-33.

Ce texte est évidemment présent à l'esprit de Danilevski lorsqu'il écrit dans *Rossija i Evropa* (1869) avec une ironie mordante à l'égard des projets d'une européisation éventuelle de l'Asie: «Ce serait des canaux, des chemins de fer sur des dizaines de milliers de verstes, pour ne rien dire des télégraphes: quel glorieux far East se dévoilerait dans une lointaine perspective!».[18] On aurait des Etats-Unis d'Europe orientale ou d'Asie occidentale, dirigés en fait, ajoute Danilevski, par les Anglais ou les Américains, «nos véritables civilisateurs européens». Bien entendu Danilevski rejette absolument un pareil programme et s'en tient au panslavisme européen.

Dostoïevski a bien Danilevski, probablement d'abord par l'intermédiaire de Strakhov, ancien camarade de Danilevski à l'Université de St. Pétersbourg en 1843. Celui-ci fréquenta le cercle de Pétrachevski, mais échappa à toute condamnation.En 1869 c'est encore Strakhov qui fit paraître *Rossija i Evropa* dans la nouvelle revue *L'Aurore* (*Zaria*). Dostoïevski réagit aussitôt, comme je l'ai rappelé dans l'article de *Dostoevsky Studies*, et invita Danilevski à Staraïa Roussa dans premiers mois de 1872, puis encore une fois un an plus tard.[19] Est-ce par Danilevski que Dostoïevski a connu l'existence du livre d'Henri Martin? Certes le nom du Français n'apparaït pas dans *Rossija i Evropa*, mais on le trouve, associé au moins par proximité à celui de Danilevski, dans une liste de *nužnye knigi*, de livres nécessaires, dressée par Dostoïevski pour l'année 1876.[20] En ce qui concerne *Rossija i Evropa*, il s'agit évidemment d'une relecture, puisque Dostoïevski avait écrit son sentiment, fort chaleureux, sur ce livre dès 1869: peut-etre, mais ce n'est pas sûr, est-ce aussi le cas pour *La Russie et l'Europe* d'Henri Martin.

Le plus étonnant est que Dostoïevski, à peu près entièrement d'accord avec les vues panslavistes de Danilevski jusqu'en 1878, se prend d'un intérêt subit pour la «mission civilisatrice de la Russie en Asie», selon les propres termes du *Journal d'un Ecrivain* de 1881.[21] Ce point de vue nouveau, totalement en contradiction avec les vues de Danilevski, coïncide au contraire précisément avec l'idée exprimée par Henri Martin, dont le nom est mentionné en 1876 par Dostoïevski, soit dix ans après la publication du livre. Ce qui n'est pas nouveau en revanche, c'est l'attention crispée que Dostoïevski porte sur l'image que l'Europe se fait de la Russie. Déjà en 1863, nous l'avons vu, il ressentait vivement la conviction ancrée chez les Polonais que leur civilisation, toute

---

18 N. J. D a n i l e v s k i j, *Rossija i Evropa*, SPb 1889, p. 64-65.

19 M. C a d o t, op. cit., p. 22-23.

20 F. M. D o s t o e v s k i j, *P. S. S*, t. 27, Léningrad 1984, p. 113 et comm. p. 377.

21 Ibid., p. 37..

occidentale, était infiniment supérieure aux moeurs asiatiques de la Russie. A travers tout le *Journal d'un Ecrivain.* Dostoïevski reproduit avec amertume les convictions qu'il pouvait trouver à cet égard chez Custine, chez Mickiewicz, chez Michelet, chez Henri Martin, et en partie chez Herzen. Il fait parler les Européens en 1876:

> Qui sont-ils, ces Russes? Des Asiates, des Tatars? [...] Le pire est que nous devions nous avouer à nous-mêmes que ce n'est pas cela. Et cependant ils sont si peu semblables à nous [...] La solution à laquelle ils s'arrêtent est taillée à leur aune, c'est celle d'hier, celle de toujours: «Ce que cela annonce, c'est la conquête, la rapine, l'astuce, la perfidie, la destruction future de la civilisation, la horde mongole unie, les Tatars».[22]

L'aventure asiatique, telle que Dostoïevski la voit dans le *Journal* de 1881, permettra enfin aux Russes de liquider leur terrible complexe d'infériorité vis-à vis de l'Europe:

> En Europe, nous avons été des ramasse-miettes et des esclaves: en Asie nous serons des seigneurs, en Europe nous avons été des Tatars, en Asie nous serons à notre tour des Européens.[23]

Et ces mots, qui annoncet le panmongolisme et l'eurasisme, étudiés entre autres par E. Lo Gatto, G. Nivat, et ici même par J. Bonamour:[24]

> Le Russe n'est pas seulement un Européen, mais aussi Asiatique [...] C'est peut-être l'Asie qui est, dans nos destins à venir, notre principale issue.[25]

Ce que Henri Martin écrivait en 1866 pour détourner la Russie de la Pologne et donc de l'Europe, Dostoïevski le redit en 1880 parce que le rêve panslaviste s'est écroulé depuis le Congrès de Berlin, et que l'Europe, selon lui, persiste à voir dans la Russie une puissance toujours aussi barbare, plus asiatique

---

[22] F. M. Dostoïevski, *Récits* etc. Pléiade, p. 673.

[23] Ibid. p. 1462.

[24] J. Bonamour *Entre les massianismes slavophiles et les Eurasiens: remarques sur K. Leont'ev,* dans Messianisme et Slavophilie, p. 199-206.

[25] F. M. Dostoïevski, *Récits* etc., Pléiade, p. 1456.

qu'européenne. Lorsque l'Europe cessa de craindre l'invasion russe, elle se forgea un nouveau mythe, le fameux péril jaune. La double menace conjuguée, russe et asiatique, cette fois sous l'étendard de la révolution, reparaît avec force dans *Les Scythes* de Blok[26]: au panmongolisme succède un eurasisme révolutionnaire, dont les effets mondiaux commencent tout juste à s'atténuer. La lutte décisive que prophétisait Henri Martin entre les Aryens (les Européens) et les Touraniens (les Moscovites alliés aux Tartares) cette nouvelle guerre de Troie n'aura peut-être pas lieu.

---

26 Voir les références dans *Dostoevsky Studies*, vol. 7, 1986, note 50, p. 33.

Andrzej Walicki — University of Notre Dame

Catholicism and the Eastern Church in Russian Religious and Philosophical Thought

The Westernization of Russia is usually associated with the secularization of Russian culture and with the emergence and development of a westernized and secularised enlightened stratum. It is often forgotten in this connection that Westernization also covered the Russian Church. Contrary to the prevailing opinion, the Church was not in the least an unshakable bulwark of the Old Russian Orthodox tradition, saved by some miracle from the destructive pressure of Westernizing reforms. On the contrary, the Westernization of orthodox spirituality began long before Peter the Great and continued until at least the early nineteenth century. Father Georges Florovsky, the best expert in Russian theology, wrote about the nearly total separation of the Orthodox secular clergy from the authentic tradition of Eastern Christianity, which was being preserved only in remote hermitages and monasteries that cultivated ascetic contemplation at the cost of completely turning away from "the matters of this world".[1] That separation weighed heavily on the history of Russian religious thought in the nineteenth and twenteenth century. It is, therefore, worth while to present briefly its causes and its forms.

The first contact between the Orthodox Christianity and the Western denominations took place of course on the territory of the Polish-Lithuanian State (formed by the Union of Lublin in 1569). The Orthodox Church saw the principal enemy in Roman Catholicism, especially in its Eastern rite, established at the Union of Brest (1596), and hence the Orthodox opponents to that union did not at first hesitate to form a common front with the Protestants.[2] That however, was merely a temporary trend, because it soon appeared that the refutation of "Latinism" by Protestant polemists also undermined the dogmatic foundations of the Orthodox Church. Therefore, the tactical alliance with the

1 Cf. G. F l o r o v s k y, *Puti russkogo bogosloviia*, Paris 1937, pp. 97-114.

2 G. F l o r o v s k y, *Western Influences in Russian Theology*, in idem: Collected Works, Belmont 1975, vol. 4, pp. 162-63.

Reformation proved irreconcilable in the long run with the maintaining and consolidation of the identity of the Eastern Church. The necessity of defending that Church against Roman Catholicism required, however, the proving of its own cause, which tempted that Church to polemize with the Roman Catholics by using their own weapon, that is, to resort to theological scholastic argumentation. Pyotr Mohyla, the metropolitan bishop of Kiev, decided to follow that path. The Spiritual Academy at Kiev, which he founded, became a bastion of resistance against the union. The Orthodox Church regained its legal status within the State, but that took place at the price of the "Latinization" of the Orthodox Christianity. As Florovsky wrote, Latinization covered not only the language, theology, and manners, but entire religious psychology as well.[3]

The cause of this phenomenon can be explained by one of the most characteristic features of the Orthodox religious consciousness, namely its orientation which might be termed mystical and existential and which is diametrically opposed to the rationalistic and existential and which prevails in Roman Catholicism. In the Eastern tradition there was no sharp distinction between mysticism and theology, between a personal experience of divine mysteries and dogmatics.[4] Nor did it recognize any clear demarcation line between theology as taught by the Church and broadly interpreted religious philosophy.[5] The mystical theology of the Eastern Church was existential in character, for its point was to help the believers to experience union with God, such an experience being not intellectual but integral, embracing the whole human being. It was programmatically antirationalistic, apophatic, that is one which defines God only by negation, which contemplates Him in His unknowability and treats the mysteries of faith as unspeakable and not accessible to human reason.[6] It did not accept the passage from the symbol to logical argumentation, from synthetic perception to conceptual analysis, and thus did not produce its own scholasticism.[7] The boundaries of scholasticism were the boundaries of the Western world. It was no wonder, therefore, that Orthodox Christianity did not know how to defend itself in contact with Roman Catholic

---

3 Ibid., p. 164

4 Cf. V. L o s s k y, *The Mystical Theology of the Eastern Churche*, London 1957, pp. 8-9.

5 Cf. J. K l i n g e r, *O istocie prawoslawia*, On the Essence Of Orthodox Chritianity, Warsaw 1983, p.149.

6 V. L o s s k y, pp. 31-32, 39 and 238. See also P. E v d o k i m o v, *L'Orthodoxie*, Paris 1959, pp. 174 and J. P e l i k a n, *The Sririt of Eastern Christendom*, Chicago and London, 1974, (Vol .2 of his The Christian Tradition), pp. 30-32, 54-55 and 258-59.

7 Cf. Y. C o n g a r, *After Nine Hundred Years. Yhe Backaground of the Schism Between the Eastern and Western Churches*, New York: 1959, pp. 40-41.

scholasticism, and when it learned how to defend itself, that is, when it produced a scholasticism of its own, it in a sense denied its own essence and became similar to the adversary it opposed.

The evolution of Orthodox Christianity which took place within the Polish-Lithuanian Commonwealth repeated itself on a larger scale in Russia under the impact of the reforms of Peter the Great. This reformer of Russia personally sided with Lutheranism as a religion which recognizes the unconditional superiority of the secular authority. That was why, assisted in this by Theophanes Prokopovich, educated in the Academy of Kiev, he did not rest satisfied with the abolition of the patriarchate and its replacement by the secular institution of the synod, but also tried to base Orthodox Church schools on Lutheran patterns.

This, however, failed, and the Roman Catholic orientation, represented by Bishop Stepan Iavorsky, also shaped in the circle of Kiev culture, gained the upper hand. This marked the large scale "Latinization" of Orthodox Church schools in Russia. The curricula in the seminaries were based on the Kiev pattern, all the subjects, including theology, were taught in Latin, often from the same handbooks which were used in Roman Catholic seminaries.[8] As Florovsky wrote, people even thought in Latin, although they prayed in Church Slavonic. That "Latinization" at the same time meant Ukrainization, and indirectly Polonization, because nearly all higher clergy were brought from the Kiev metropolis. The native Russian population treated the seminaries as a kind of unwanted Latin-Polish colony on the Russian soil.[9]

This process, which went on for a whole century, resulted in a farreaching "westernization", or "latinization" of the Russian Orthodox Church. It is true that it was a non-organic process, which artificially combined heterogeneous cultural elements.[10] Nevertheless it ran deep and was quite effective in cutting off the Russian Church from its spiritual sources.

The rediscovery of the Orthodox spirituality took place in the nineteenth century, as a part of an intensive search for defining Russian national identity. It is significant that most of these atttempts at self-definition had to revolve around the problem of the relationship between the Orthodox Church and the Roman Church. There is no exaggeration in saying that Catholicism became an important frame of reference for the great debate on the meaning of Russian destiny.The ideas of such thinkers as Peter Chaadaev, The Slavophiles, Fedor Dostoevsky and Vladimir Soloviev provide an ample illustration of this thesis.

---

8 See G. F l o r o v s k y, *The Orthodox Church and the Ecumenical Movement Prior to 1910,* in idem: Collected Works, Vol. 2, p. 186.

9 Ibid., vol. 4, pp. 166-67.

10 Florovsky called that process using Sprengler's term pseudomorphosis, ibid., Vol. 2, p. 181.

1. Chaadaev, or Negative Self-Definition.

The first thoroughly conceived answer to the question of the meaning of being Russian was negative in character: It defined Russia not in affirmative but in negative terms, not by what it was, but by what is was not. I mean, of course, the famous Philosophical Letter by Petr Chaadaev, the Russian disciple of the French traditionalists.

According to Chaadaev, Russia had no history. He meant by this that Russian history was merely a collection of meaningless events, lacking the continuity of tradition and the unity of purpose. It was so, he argued, because of Russias's separation from the universal Church, the Church of Rome, the history-making force of Christianity. True, the Russians were Christians, but so were the Ethiopians; in both cases religious affiliation did not ensure membership in the Christian civilisation. The European nations were marching through the centuries hand in hand. They fought together to free the Holy Sepulchre and prayed to God in one and the same language. The history of the West was sacred history, the kingdom of God had to some extent already materialized in Europe. In contrast with this, Russia was a handicapped country, forgotten by Providence and not covered by the "universal education of humankind". Owing to this the Russians had no guidelines and support in their past, lived without fixed customs and rules for anything, knew nothing about the idea of duty, justice, right and order. "Western syllogism" — logic and methodical thinking — was completely alien to thier undisciplined minds. Small wonder that they grow but do not mature, that "not a single useful thought has sprouted in the sterile soil" of their country.

The impression evoked by publication of the Philosophical Letter was erroneous and almost completely negative. Nikolai Yazykov in a rhymed pamphlet called Chaadaev a traitor, a "proud slave of everything alien", ready to kiss the shoes of the Pope. The Emperor decided that Chaadaev be treated as a madman and subjected to compulsory supervision by physicians and the police. This explains the title of Chaadaev's text The Apology of a Madman, in which he tried to modify his view of Russia by asserting that the lack of history could be interpreted not as a disaster but as a great chance.

However, from the point of view of the present paper another modification of Chaadaev's views seems to be more important. Namely, his change of the one-sidedly negative attitude towards the Orthodox Church. This more balanced view is best developed in Chaadaev's Fragments et pensées diverses, recently published by the Japanese scholar Tsuguo Togawa.[11]

---

[11] See P. T s c h a a d a e v, *Fragments et pensées diverses*, Presentés par Tsuguo Togawa, Slavic Studies, No. 23, pp. 32-33.

The Western Church, Chaadaev argued, was called to make history. It was ambitious, intolerant, and did not despise the goods of this world, but all that was as it were the reverse side of the sublime misson which it carried out in the social history of mankind. The calling of the Eastern Church was quite different. That Church, which "lived in solitude prepared for it by barbarity", developed the contemplative and aspect ascetic of Christianity, and hence all forms of secular ambitions were forbidden to it as being incompatible with its inner essence. It this way the author of Philosophical Letters arrived at the conception of the equal status of the Roman Catholic and the Orthodox Church as the two poles of the absolute truth. On the one side there was "activism" and "sociality", on the other, contemplation, ascesis, and the Evangelical purity of Christ's teachings.[12] As we shall see, very similar, if not identical views, were developed later by the great religious philosopher, Vladimir Soloviev.

As can easily be noted, the new conception substantiated *ex post facto* what could be treated as an inconsistency on Chaadaev's part at the time when he was writing his Philosophical Letters: the fact that he did not consider it necessary formally to join the Church of Rome. Moreover, that conception could serve as an instrument of criticism of the above described process of the "Latinization" of Orthodox Christianity, and also as a springboard for the idealization of monastic Orthodox Christianity of mystical ascetics, the *startsy*, and hermits, Orthodox Christianity not contaminated by Latin influence.

But there is also no doubt that Chaadaev did not stop thinking about the Kingdom of God as realised in history, in the world, and that he saw the Church as its historical incarnation. It is also striking that while he now saw that in the controversy between Roman Catholicism and Orthodox Christianity there were arguments on both sides, his firmly negative attitude towards Protestantism remained unchanged. If we add to this the highest idea of universal unity, an idea to which he was unshakably faithful, then we find it difficult to question the hypothesis that the modification of his opinions led Chaadaev to his seeing the religious future of the world as the union of the Eastern Church with the Western Church. Note that such a union was supposed by him to take place on equal rights, with the due recognition of the separate tasks of both Churches in the past.

2. Slavophiles, or Affirmative Self-Definition.

The ideology of Slavophiles was in a sense a reply to Chaadaev's views, as its complex structure and its different variants. I shall try instead to summa-

---

12 P. Y. C h a a d a e v, *Sochinieniia i pis'ma*, ed. by N. Gershenzon, Moscow 1913, Vol. 1, p. 254.

rize the Slavophile conception of the contrast between the Roman and Eastern Church.

To put it briefly, the Slavophile doctrine was a reversal of Chaadaev's view of the effects of Russia's separation from the Roman Catholic Church. For the Slavophiles this seperation was not a handicap but a real blessing of fortune. The Roman Church, they argued, has inherited the rationalism and juridical spirit of ancient Rome and, therefore, followed the path of the juridicization and rationalization of faith. As a result, it replaced the organic commmunity of living tradition by codified legal conventions, renounced living faith as dangerous mysticism, and separated dogmas from living experience by trying to prove them by means of rational arguments of scholasticism. In contrast to this, the Orthodox Church, not having inherited the fatal legacy of Rome, could preserve Christ's teaching, and the tradition of the first six centuries of Christianity, in a form uncontaminated by rationalism. It did not produce its own scholastic theology because it knew well that the content of religious faith cannot be formulated in a conceptual system. Its conception of the Church, and all other forms of a truly Christian community, was based upon the principle of "sobornost" , that is a freely accepted, non-rationalized, living unity, excluding both the Catholic "unity without freedom" and the Protestant "freedom without unity". Aleksei Khomiakov, the main representative of the Slavovophile ecclesiology, added to this a pneumatic dimension: he saw the essence of the Church "neither in institution nor in doctrine", but in the charismatic community of tradition that covers all the faithful.[13]

As can easily be seen, such an interpretation of Christianity and such a vision of the Church were deeply rooted in the old tradition of the apopathic theology of the Eastern Church. By the same token, they were strongly, although not explicitly, critical of the process of "Latinization" which took place within the Russian Church. For tactical reason the Slavophile thinkers did not stress this but, nonetheless, the Orthodox hierarchs were all aware of it. This resulted in a fact which has an ironic meaning: Khomiakov's theological works had to be printed abroad (mostly in French), and their distribution in Russia was strongly prohibited.

In the long run, however, the Slavophiles's call for a 'spiritual awakening' through return to the sources of a distinctively Eastern tradition in Christianity became the main inspiration of the trend of renewal in Russian

---

[13] See Father A. Pawlowski, *Idea Kościoła w ujęciu rosyjskiej teologii i historiozofii*, The Idea of Church as Interpreted in Russian Theology and Historiosophy, Warsaw 1935, S. Bolshakoff, *The Doctrine of the Unity of the Church in the Works of Khomyakov and Moehler*, London 1946.

Orthodox thought and brought about a significant change in the self-consciousness of the Orthodox Church. Sergei Bulgakov, Georges Florovsky, Vladimir Lossky, Paul Evdokimov and other Russian theologians of the 20th century demonstrated that the Slavophiles were right in such issues as the anti-intellectualism and anti-individualism of the Eastern Church, its lack of scholastic tradition and of the striving for a doctrinal synthesis, the focal status of ecclesiology, and orientation towards Old Chistianity. In many cases, the convergence between the most eminent representatives of Orthodox theology in the 20th century and Slavophile thought is somewhat alarming. If, for instance, Father Georges Florovsky defines true "catholicity" in the same way as Khomiakov did — by equating it with sobornost': if he opposes to one another two types of consciousness: individualistic consciousness and "catholic" consciousness (in the sense of Khomiakov's s o b o r n o s t 'soznaniia'): and if he finally defines the Church as "the unity of charismatic life", based on tradition conceived as a charismatic, and not merely historical, principle[14], than we have to see in that not so much a confirmation of Khomiakov's ideas, but rather a manifestation of their direct influence.

The greatest exponent of the Slavophile ideas in Russian literature was, of course, Fedor Dostoevsky. His views are too complex and, perhaps, too contradictory to be briefly dealt with in this paper: Therefore, I shall limit myself to two remarks on his contribution to the great Russian debate on the relation between Roman-Catholic and East-Orthodox spirituality.

First, Dostoevsky followed the Slavophiles in seeing Catholocism as the ultimate source of all evils of the West.[15] In his view, the legacy of ancient Roman Empire transformed the Roman Church into a kind of authoritarian and imperialistc state, replacing the inner bonds of common faith by purely external means of unification and trying to save mankind not by Christ, but by violence. From this perspective, Protestantism appeared to be a legitimate protest of the atomized consciousness against the external authority of the Church, while modern socialism appeared as a new edition of the Catholic "unity without freedom". Hence Dostoevsky's obsessive fears that Catholics might embrace socialism and socialists recognize the authority of the Roman Pope. These fears found expression in his prophetic masterpiece The Legend of the Grand Inquisitor, showing thereby that religious and political prejudices can be sometimes intellectually and artistically fruitful.

---

[14] See F l o r o v s k y, *Bible, Church, Tradition* in his Collected Works, Vol. 1, pp. 39-47.

[15] See A. W a l i c k i, *The Slavophile Controversy*, Oxford 1975, pp. 540-43 and idem: *A History of Russian Thought. From the Enlightenment to Marxism*, Stanford Calif., 1979, pp. 317-20.

Secondly, it is significant that in his struggle against Western ideas Dostoevsky never opposed them with logical argumentation. His decisive argument was always negative in character, an argument *a contrario*, based on showing the consequences of its rejection. Thus, for instance, in the Legend logical arguments are left to the Inquisitor while Christ vindicates his truth without resorting to reason and word, It seems that we can see in it the influence (if not direct than indirect at least) of the tradition of the apophatic, negative theology which claimed that divine truth escapes rational definitions, that one can only say what it is not, but cannot formulate what it positively is. This has been noticed by Sergius Hessen when he wrote that "the philosophy of The Brothers Karamazov comes close directly to the tradition of negative theology".[16] If this is so, then we would have to treat this as probably the most important proof of the thesis that there was a profound relationship between Dostoevsky's *Weltanschauung* and the rewakening of the Eastern Christian spirituality which took place in nineteenth-century Russia.

3. Vladimir Soloviev, or an Attempt at Reconciliation.

Vladimir Soloviev, a friend admirer of Dostoevsky who was to become the greatest philosopher of nineteenth-century Russia, started his philosophical career as a disciple of the Slavophile thinkers. Further development of his views, however, consisted in his gradually disassociating himself from both the Slavophiles and Dostoevsky. This was due to his ecumenical ideas, combined with his growing liking for Roman Catholocism. In this respect he greatly resembled Petr Chaadaev.

For Soloviev, the unification of Churches meant above all the union of the Orthodox Church with the Roman Catholic Church. One can hardly resist the temptation of explaining (in part at least) this idea by his strong connections with the culture of the so called Western borderlands of Russia, that is the territories which at one time belonged to the powerful influence of Roman Catholicism. The relevant facts are as follows.

Soloviev's mother, neé Brzeski, came from a Polish gentry family which had settled in the Ukraine and was related to Grigori Skovoroda, "the Ukrainian Socrates".[17] His paternal grandfather, Mikhail Soloviev, was an Orthodox priest

---

[16] See S. H e s s e n, *Bor'ba utopii i avtonomii dobra v mirovozzrenii F. M. Dostoevskogo i Vl. Solovieva* in Sovremennyie zapiski, Paris 1931, Vol. 45, pp. 271-305 and Vol. 46, pp. 321-51. Quoted from S. H e s s e n, *Studia z filozofii kultury*, Ed. by A. Walicki, Warsaw 1968, pp. 123-24.

[17] See S. M. S o l o v i e v, *Zhizn' i tvorcheskaia evoliutsiia Vladimira Solovieva*, Brussels 1977, pp. 31-34.

educated in a seminary of the Kiev type, that is an Orthodox school which used Latin as a language of lectures and courses and was subject to the influence of Roman Catholic scholasticism. His nephew, Sergei Mikhailovich Soloviev (a Roman Catholic priest, who during the first years of Soviet Russia was in Moscow the spiritual superior of the Soviet Catholics of the Greek-Russian rite), assessed such a school differently than Father Florovsky: not as an example of an artificial and deplorable pseudomorphosis but as proof of a creative cultural osmosis. In his book on Vladimir Soloviev he mentioned proudly his personal treasure: a Latin Bible that had belonged to Mikhail Soloviev and bore the inscription *Ex libris Michael Soloviovus.*[18]

After his breaking with Slavophilism, Vladimir Soloviev became an ardent prophet of the so-called "free theocracy". It was to materialize in the unification of the human race under the spiritual rule of the Pope and the secular rule of the Russian Tsar. The books which propagated this utopian vision were received in Russia as propaganda of Roman Catholicism and for considerations of censorship had to be published abroad. Such a reception was not just a misunderstanding if we consider the fact that in 1866 Soloviev went as far as to recognize the infallibility of the pope, and three years later defended that dogma in public (In La Russie et l'Eglise Universelle). And, of course, it was not unknown that he thought very seriously about realizing his messianic vision. (He tried to win for this a Croatian bishop, Joseph Strossmayer, and through his intermediary also Pope Leo XIII. The Pope was quite impressed by Soloviev's ideal, but thought that only a miracle could make it come true.)[19]

It should be added, that Soloviev combined his theocratic utopia with a bold criticism of "historical Christianity" and of the policy of the Russian autocracy, especially on national and religious questions. In a series of articles published in the liberal Vestnik Evropy and reprinted in two volumes entitled Natsional'nyi vopros v Rossi, he firmly condemned all forms of persecution and discrimination of national and religious minorities. But he did this not only because of his acceptance of the liberal principles: for him it was also a part of his struggle for materialization of his theocratic utopia.

Let us be more specific. For Soloviev the nationality problem in Russia was above all the problem of Jews and Poles, of the difficult coexistence of Judaism, Catholicism and Orthodoxy in the western borderlands of the Empire. He saw the Russians as a "theocratic nation" but not the only one; in his eyes the Jews and the Poles were also "theocratic nations", ones which had not

---

[18] Ibid., p. 31.

[19] See K. Mochulsky, *Vladimir Soloviev. Zhizn' i uchenie*, Paris 1951, p. 185.

abandoned the Messianic hope that the truth of their faith at one time be realised in the form of social and political institutions.[20] It is resonable to suppose that Soloviev developed such an opinion of the Poles under the influence of Adam Mickiewicz's Messian ideas.[21] Anyhow, the fact that the majority of Poles and also the majority of Jews found themselves, after the partition of Poland, in the Russian Empire acquired enormous importance when seen in this perspective.

The role of the Jews and the Poles in the establishment of "free theocracy" was to be as follows. The Jews, the nation of Biblical prophets, the chosen people of the Old Testament, and now the nation of industrialists and merchants, represented the principle of materialistic (or naturalistic) and activistic individualism. Hence, it would be to the point if they held in their hands the economic life of the future theocratic empire.[22] The naturalistic elements in Judaism would guarantee that economic activity would lose the character of a pitiless exploitation of Nature and would assume the form securing a harmonious relation between Nature and humankind.

The role of Poles would, in a sense, be a continuation of their traditional mission, that is the spreading of Roman Catholicism among the Slavs. The enmity of the Poles towards the Russians, Soloviev argued, had only spiritual causes, because in the economic realm Poland experienced from Russia more good than evil. The reconciliation between Russia and Rome would eliminate the principal cause of that enmity, the more so as the Poles would play an important role of intermediaries in that reconciliation.[23] Further, Russia lacked an independent and active upper class, and that role could successfully be played by the Polish gentry, thus satisfying its social aspirations.[24] The moral satisfaction of the Poles would automatically bring about the decline of the Russian revolutionary movement, which was merely "a mask of the Polish issue". (On

---

20 See V. S. S o l o v i e v, *Evereistvo i khristiianski vopros* in idem: Sobranie sochinienii, 2nd ed. 1911-1913, phototype edition Brussels 1966, Vol. 4

21 It seems wortwhile to note that Soloviev knew both Mickiewicz's poetry and his messianic ideas, as set forth in his Paris lectures on Slavonic literature (1840-1844). In 1898, in a lecture given on the occasion of the centenary of Mickiewicz's birth, he interpreted Mickiewicz's Messianism as the victory of spiritual freedom over the external authority of the Church and, at the same time, the overcoming of nationalism by the subordination of the national cause to the cause of the universal regeneration of humankind. Cf. Soloviev, Sobranie sochinienii, Vol. 9, pp. 257-64. Mochulsky has rightly observed that the same could be said about Soloviev himself Vladimir Soloviev, p. 247.

22 Cf. S o l o v i e v, *Sobranie Sochinienii*, Vol. 4, pp. 184-85.

23 Ibid., pp. 180-82.

24 Ibid., pp. 170-80.

that point Soloviev was in agreement with the Slavophiles and Katkov for whom the Russian revolutionary movement was a result of "Polish intrigues".)

It is worth noting at this point that Soloviev was greatly interested in the Uniate rite. In order to become aquainted with the controversies over the Union of Brest he read, among other things, a 16th century treatise in Polish.[25] His attitude toward the Black Madonna of Częstochowa was a moving testimony of his endeavours to reconcile Roman Catholic Poland with Orthodox Russia. It manifested itself in his recalling the fact that the miracle-working painting now in the monastery at Jasna Góra in Częstochowa in Poland was in fact an icon from the Byzantine school, worshipped also by orthodox believers. In this way it "united in the same emotion the numberless crowds of Roman Catholic Poles and Orthodox Russians".[26]

In the early 1890's, Soloviev started losing his faith in the realisation of his theocratic utopia and as a result of that came even closer to the liberals. This marked the third period in the evolution of his views, a period in which he tried to treat philosophical problems autonomously, without linking them to religious conceptions. But the secularization of his thought did not weaken his commitment to the reconciliation of the Eastern Church with Rome. In February 1896, Soloviev received communion from Nikolai Tolstoy, an Uniate priest (who had become an Uniate under the influence of Soloviev's ideas).[27] The interpretation of that act is a controversial point. Some authors see in it merely Soloviev's belief in the theological validity of intercommunion.[28] Others notice in it something more, namely the practical application of the opinion that membership in the Eastern Church does not preclude membership in the Church of Rome because these two Churches are separated from one another only externally, and not in their internal essence.[29] Still others, mainly Roman Catholics, stress the fact that the reception of communion was preceded by the reading aloud of the Trent confession of faith and hence must be treated as tantamount to the adoption of Roman Catholicism. The opinion of S.M. Soloviev, who stated that the philosopher himself, as well as his family, interpreted the act as a conversion to Roman Catholicism, seems to be extremely important in this matter.

---

25 See S. M. Soloviev, p. 236. We should notice that Soloviev's view of the Union of Brest was different in different periods of his intellectual evolution. At the beginning it was rather negative. As late as 1883, he called it a "merely external and partial union" Ibid., p. 223.

26 See V.S. Soloviev, *Sobranie sochinienii*, Vol. 9, pp.69-70 "Pol'skaja national'naia tserkov".

27 See S. M. Soloviev, p. 346.

28 See J. Klinger, pp. 291-92.

29 Cf. Florkovsky, *Collected Works*, Vol. 2, p. 231 "The Orthodox Church and the Ecumenical Movement".

Soloviev's texts, especially his book La Russie et l'Eglise Universelle (1889) provide a similar, but not identical, answer to this question.

Like Chaadaev, Soloviev came to the conclusion that in the controversy between the Western and the Eastern Church both parties had their valid arguments. The Church of Rome did succumb to the temptation of power, but worked as a strong history-making force. The Eastern Church remained faithful to the pure teachings of Christ, but did not try to embody it into the historical world of culture. The Church of Rome committed errors but did not subordinate itself to the secular power and was active in laying the foundations of the Kingdom of God. The Eastern Church avoided the temptations of power at the price of becoming subordinated to the particular interests of the secular power, which resulted in the fact that pure Christian tradition, to which it wanted to remain faithful, was preserved in it only in the purely contemplative life of the monasteries.

In other words, the Eastern Church, like St. Cassyan in the folk legend of St. Nicholas and St. Cassyan, abstained from work being concerned about the cleanliness of his garments. The Church of Rome, like St.Nicholas, did soil his garments but showed activity and won the right to become the leader. Thus in the last analysis there were arguments on both sides, but they did not carry equal strength. St. Cassyan should recognize the leadership of St. Nicholas.

Soloviev formulated that idea quite unambiguously: "No-one asks us to change our Eastern nature nor to disavow the specific character of our religious spirit. We merely have to accept without reservation the simple truth that we, the East, are only a part of the Universal Church, and that part at that which does not have the centre in itself. This is why it is necessary for us to join our forces with the great universal centre which Providence placed in the West".

In other words, Soloviev did not proclaim that members of the Eastern Orthodox Church shuld simply convert to Roman Catholicism. He proposed rather a union of the two Churches. He did recommend an unconditional recognition of the supreme authority of the Pope, but, at the same time, strongly stressed that this should not amount to abandoning the specific traits, specific traditions, of the Eastern Church. The Roman Pope was, in his view, the head of the Universal Church, but this did not mean equating the Universal Church with the Roman Catholic Church. Universal Church was a broader notion, embracing both Western and Eastern Christianity. The Eastern Church had never ceased to be a living, legitimate part of the Universal Church. Therefore, the recognition of the authority of the Pope would greatly strengthen the Orthodox Church without entailing any danger for the existence of the distinctively Eastern religious culture.

Soloviov's own *oeuvre* was, I think, an excellent illustration of such a possibility. Fascination with Roman Catholicism harmoniously coexisted in it with a deep rootedness in the Eastern spirituality. Take, for instance, his idea of Sophia, the Eternal Wisdom of God —the central idea of his philosophical cosmology and historiosophy. He found it in the writings of the gnostics (where it is "divine matter" and "feminine aeson"),in Boehme (who identified it with "eternal virginity"), in Swedenborg, Saint-Martin and Baader, but he thought - and was right in doing so —that it was particularly close to the traditions of Eastern Christianity. Anyhow, it was so in his philosophy. In order to understand the functioning of the idea of Sophia in his system one has to associate it with the conception of non-created divine energies which is typical of the apophatic theology of the Eastern Church. In an interesting manuscript Sofia (1876), Soloviev unambiguously declared himself in favor of apophatic theology: the essence of God, he stated, is not subject to definition because it is not a being but the principle of all being, and hence "non-being" or "super-being". It followed that the essence of God was completely inaccessible to man. But one could not stop at this because the very goal of theology (as was the case in apophatic theology) was defined as participation in divine nature. This gave rise to the problem of reconciling the inaccessibility of God with His accessibility, a problem which was solved by the conception of non-created energies through which God manifests Himself to man. Sophia was for Soloviev just such a divine energy (and perhaps even the totality of those energies): it was divinity in the world, unity of the created world, and the link between the world and transcendent and inaccessible God. Thus, the concept of Sophia enabled Soloviev to reconcile transcendence with immanence, to sanctify matter, and preach the idea of religious rehabilitation and "deification" of Nature. And this, of course, was a theological foundation of his theory of uniting the divine and the human in the institutions of "free theocracy".

Unlike most Polish philosophers of the Romantic period, Soloviev did not set himself the task of creating a programmatically national philosophy. He emphasized rather the universality of his ideas. In spite of this, however, it is undeniable that his philosophy was deeply rooted in Russian national culture and that its practical conclusions were a form of Russian national and religious Messianism. If the Slavs, and the Russians in particular, are called to reconcile the East with the West and to build the Kingdom of God on the earth in the form of "free theocracy", then, *eo ipso*, the philosophy that substantiates that mission of theirs is both universal and specifically Russian. It is Russian because it serves the historical mission of the Russian nation: it is universal because that mission is universal. Let it be noted in this connection that Soloviev realized perfectly well that religious Messianism, even if closely linked to national Messianism, required the renunciation of national particularism. He illustrated that idea by referring to the evolution of Mickiewicz's Messianism.

The Russian character of Soloviev's philospohy was not merely intendent by him; it was also an unquestionable fact. His idea that "the point is not to thwart our religious and moral individuality, but to add new elements to it and to make it live an universal and progresive life", must be interpreted not as a declaration in favor of linking the Orthodox Church to the Church of Rome, but also as a manifestation of his intention to preserve the Orthodox Russian "religious and moral individuality". We have seen he was consistent in that striving in his conception of Sophia, which intentionally referred to the mystical traditions of Eastern Christianity. The same applies to his declaration in favor of apophatic theology, his Old Christian orientation in accordance with the spirit of Orthodox Christianity, and to his criticism of Western rationalism that was to a large extent aimed also at the rationalism of Roman Catholic scholasticism and the juridical and rationalistic character of the dominant trend in Roman Catholic ecclesiology. As a critic of one-sided rationalism Soloviev closely followed the ideas of the Slavophiles and Dostoevsky — although, of course, he resolutely rejected their nationalistic extremism and anti-Catholic prejudices. In his positive ideal of "free theocracy" he was also very close to the Slavophile *'sobornost'*.

Soloviev's fascination with Roman Catholicism should be seen in a variety of contexts: above all, in the context of the "Latin" influence within the Orthodox Church and in the context of pro-Catholic and anti-Catholic attitudes in Russian religious and social thought. It seems justified to say that confrontation with Catholicism proved to be very fruitful for the Russian thinkers. It was a powerful catalyst in the development of religious philisophy in nineteenth-century Russia. It was characteristic and significant that this philosophy begins with Chaadaev, an enthusiast of the Catholic religion and culture, and achieves its climax in Soloviev —another admirer of the Church of Rome. Equally important is the fact that even the Slavophiles, whose attitude towards Catholicism was extremely defensive and hostile, developed their theories in opposition to Catholicism, which resulted in a form of negative dependence — a dependence that stems from the polemical attitude. By providing them with a "negative frame of reference", Catholicism enabled the Slavophiles to discover the originality of the semi-forgotten spiritual traditions of the Eastern Christianity, thus paving the way for Russia's "theological awakening". Vladimir Soloviev made another long step in this direction.

Lucjan Suchanek — Université Jagellonne, Cracovie

Les idées vraies et les idées fausses: de la théorie de Paul Morozov

En 1872, dans l'imprimerie moscovite de Bachmiettev, est publié un opuscule intitulé "Coup d'oeil sur la génèse et l'évolution des fausses conceptions de la liberté" (Wzglad na načalo i razvitie prevratnych poniatij o svobode).[1] Les initiales P.M. sous lesquelles se cachait l'auteur, permettent de dire aujourd'hui, grâce au dictionnaire des pseudonymes de I. Massanov[2], qu'il s'agissait de Pavel Timofieievitch Morozov (1805-1881)[3], écrivain et savant, auteur d'ouvrages en histoire et en météorologie.[4]

Les idées de Morozow présentées dans cette brochure doivent être situées parmi les idéologies réactionnaires apparues en Russie dans les dernières décennies du XIXème siècle. La notion "réactionnaire" est empruntée à A. Walicki, en tant que "définition descriptive selon laquelle une idéologie donnée exprime des idéaux rétrospectifs, idéalisant (directement ou non) les étapes vécues de l'évolution sociale.[5]

Parmi les penseurs et les publicistes que l'on pourrait considérer comme, du moins sur certains points, de Morozov, nous devons mentionner N. Danilevski, K. Pobiedonoscev, K. Leontiev. L'auteur du "Coup d'oeil" n'atteint cependant ni leur niveau de réflexion ni leur profondeur théorique. Chez Morozov

---

1 *Wzglad na naczało i razwitije priewratnych poniatij o swobodie*, Soczinienije P. M, Moskwa 1872.

2 I. M a s a n o w, *Słowar' psiewdonimow russkich pisatielej, uczenych i obszczestwiennych diejatielej w czetyriech tomach.* T. 2. (K-P), Moskwa 1957, s. 321.

3 Les brèves biographies de Morozov comportent: *Enciklopiediczeskij słowar*, T. XIX, SPb 1896, s. 873; *Bolszaja enciklopiedija*, pod ried. S. Jużakowa, T. XIII, SPb 1903, s. 403.

4 *Travaux historiques, littéraires, mémoires: Istorija Odiessy*, Odiesskij Almanach na 1831; *Bor'ba christianstwa s jazyczestwom*, Moskwitianin 1845, cz. III; *Arabieski iz mira duchowno-prawosawnogo*, SPb 1874; *Moje znakomstwo s M. L. Magnickim*, Moskwa 1877; *Tri siemji.* Rasskaz. Moskwa 1872; *Iz odiesskich wospominanij*, Russkij Archiw, 1877; *Dieriewienskije biesiady* 1880; *Soczinienija P. M. Morozowa*, Moskwa 1883.

5 A. W a l i c k i, *Rosyjska filizofia i myśl społeczna od Oświecenia do marksizmu*, Warszawa 1973, p. 424.

nous retrouvons certains aspects présents déjà dans la doctrine slavophile classique, notamment il y est question de la crise de la civilisation européenne. Cette analyse est d'ailleurs quelque peu simplifieé et modifiée chez Morozov. Walicki explique ce phénomène de la manière suivante: "Deux points revêtent une importance décisive: premièrement, le mouvement révolutionnaire, et comme conséquence — la nécessité de forger une arme idéologique contre le nihilisme; deuxièmement, l'activation du mouvement polonais visant l'indépendance, mouvement qui termine avec l'insurrection de 1863 et qui entraîne une explosion du chauvinisme. La Russie est alors envahie par une vague de nationalisme et de réaction anti-nihiliste, par des idées slavophiles qui, vulgarisées et vidées de leur contenu anti-capitaliste, ont été absorbées, et comme jamais auparavant, popularisées par le journalisme réactionnaire apportant ainsi une nuance particulière au monarchisme officiel, comme d'ailleurs également à d'autres versions de l'idéologie nationaliste".[6]

La modification et l'actualisation de la doctrine slavophile ont fait en quelque sorte l'affaire de la monarchie absolue, étant l'expression du nationalisme et de l'impérialisme. Selon la périodisation proposée par A. Walicki, la théorie de Morozov se situerait dans la troisième période (après 1861), époque, où "s'entremêlent le mouvement slavophile et le panslavisme (...), et où le panslavisme devient une force politique réelle".[7]

Les idées de Morozov ont aussi une dimension religieuse.

Au début nous trouvons une sorte d'épigraphie: "L'existence spirituelle et matérielle possèdent un principe qui les unit: Dieu. Tout vient de lui, tout existe par lui et pour lui. En Dieu sont la clarté et la force, le bien et la bonté. L'homme vit de la vie qu'il a reçue de Dieu. Plus ses liens avec Dieu sont nombreux, plus sa perfection est grande" (p. 1).

L'idée centrale de cet épigraphe: "tout vient de lui, tout existe par lui et pour lui" a été empruntée à la lettre de Saint Paul aux Romains (ch. 11, v. 36).[8]

La conception historiciste de l'évolution de l'humanité, évolution comprise comme une succession d'époques de civilisations et systèmes d'états, a été fondée sur l'opposition entre la raison individuelle et la raison divine, entre la volonté individuelle et la volonté suprême. L'union complète de ces éléments devait garantir l'harmonie du cosmos primitif et signifiait une parfaite concor-

---

6 A. W a l i c k i, *W kręgu konserwatywnej utopii*, Warszawa 1964, p. 380.

7 Ibid., p. 402.

8 *Cité d'après La Bible*. Ancien et Nouveau Testament. Alliance Biblique Universelle 1984, p. 229.

dance des pensées et des désirs. Tel était le statut éthique de l'Eden, dont l'ordre a été perturbé par la Chute. L'Ecriture Sainte voit dans la Chute, celle des anges comme celle des hommes, la cause de la dysharmonie. L'histoire de l'humanité a toutefois connu d'autres étapes, postérieures, qui dans une perspective théléologique, doivent mener à une nouvelle harmonie. "Sans l'Eden biblique, sans le Golgotha et sans la trompette du jugement dernier — écrit Morozov — l'histore n'est qu'un amas d'actions sans plan et sans but". (p. 32)

La chute des anges a été la conséquence d'un abus de liberté et de la conviction que l'on peut atteindre la perfection de ses propres forces. Il en a été de même avec l'homme, qui a voulu se fier à sa propre raison et à sa volonté, provoquant aussi la destruction du lien avec la source divine de la vie et de la clarté. L'homme a choisi la voie d'une autonomie illusoire, a cherché son bonheur dans la raison, ce qui devait entraîner une repture la science humaine et la sagesse de Dieu. Morozov constate: "Dans la science da la structure de l'état, cette rupture se traduit par des idées fausses sur la liberté". (p. 5)

Quant à la caractéristique des systèmes étatiques, la théorie de Morozov est centrée sur la notion de liberté. Morozov propose une vision antinomique de ce problème: le mode antique (Grèce, Rome, Israël), et le mode chrétien. Avec le christianisme, écrit-il, "les anciennes et fausses conceptions de la liberté ont été remplacées par de nouvelles conceptions, vraies, cette fois-ci".(p. 7). La chretienté proclamait le thèse selon laquelle la liberté, de même que le pouvoir, provient de Dieu. La liberté doit se manifester à travers le pouvoir, c'est-à-dire que le pouvoir a besoin de la liberté d'action.

Morozov prône une conception de l'Etat fondé sur la religion, état qui garantit un ordre socio-juridique en sanctionnant le pouvoir et la liberté. Les principes d'un tel Etat ne peuvent pas être inventés, puisque la réalité morale, comme d'ailleurs la réalité physique, possède ses lois propres et immuables, lois, que la volonté de l'homme n'est pas en mesure de transformer. Ce que l'homme doit faire, c'est découvrir ces lois, mais non les créer. Les lois inventées par l'homme ont toujours provoqué des dommages, un affaiblissement de la foi et de la moralité.

Les constitutions des peuples antiques étaient bâties sur des lois religieuses, chez les Juifs, les principes avaient été introduits par Moïse. "C'est sur eux, écrit Morozov, qu'il a été possible de construire l'édifice de la vraie monarchie, venant du Roi-Prophète. Cette monarchie, empruntée aux Israélites, a pu renaître au temps de Constantin Ier, pour passer ensuite en Russie, où elle devra se développer pour les bienfaits des peuples". (p. 11). L'essence d'une telle monarchie c'est l'amour, la confiance et l'obéissance qui impliquent l'unité du pouvoir et de la nation, de même que l'unité du pouvoir religieux et laïque.

Cette forme de pensée religieuse et politique trouve ses racines dans l'idée byzantine du parallélisme du monarque et de Dieu.[9] Un écrivain byzantin, le diâcre Agapet, dans son oeuvre "Avertissements à l'empereur Justinien" (Ekthesis)[10], tout en prônant l'idée de l'union des intérêts de l'Empire et de l'Eglise, disait que le pouvoir royal n'est pas autonome mais qu'il est un don de Dieu, et c'est pourquoi il faut qu'il soit soumis à l'ordre moral qui provient de ce même Dieu. S. Runciman en analysant la théocratie byzantine, fondée sur le principe de la mimésis — imitation, constate que dans l'Empire byzantin "la constitution, pour se servir d'un terme purement juridique, était un reflet du royaume céleste (...). Comme Dieu règne dans les cieux, de même le souverain créé à son image, doit régner sur la terre et remplir les commandements de Dieu".[11]

La conception de Morozov du pouvoir de l'empereur et de l'Etat tenait bien évidemment compte de toutes ces métamorphoses et de tous ces ajustemenst que devait subir l'idée de sacralisation du monarque sur le sol russe, sol, sur lequel il fallait ajouter à la motivation théologique une motivation politique. Dans l'ouvrage de Jivov et d'Uspienski nous pouvons lire: "Les prémisses politiques de la sacralisation du monarque ont été instaurées selon deux tendances: d'une part le fait de reporter sur le tsar moscovite la fonction du basileus byzantin — ce qui a conduit à la conception de Moscou-Rome III, comme c'était le cas de l'optique qui en était issue, à savoir l'influence byzantine sur la vie étatique et religieuse de la Russie (133 partir du règne d'Alexis Michailovitch); d'autre part, et ce à partir du règne de Pierre Ier, le tsar est devenu le chef de l'Eglise.[12]

Dans l'approche historiciste de Morozov, l'évolution des formes du pouvoir et de l'Etat menait à la formation d'une structure suprême, c'est-à-dire à la monarchie orthodoxe russe. Cette idée restait en contradiction avec la conception de P. Tchaadaev, exprimée dans sa "Première Lettre Philosophique". A la recherche du Royaume de Dieu sur terre, ce penseur a tout d'abord été fasciné par le catholicisme. Sur ce point nous pouvons constater chez lui une influence des idées théocratiques de Joseph de Maistre et de Bonald. En même temps, "l'orthodoxie lui apparaissait comme trop passive et peu historique".[13] Ce n'est

---

9 Voir: W. Ż i w o w, B. U s p i e n s k i j, *Car i Bog. Semioticzeskije aspekty sakralizacii monarcha w Rossii*, In: Jazyki kultury i problema pieriewodimosti, ed. B. Uspienskij, Moskwa 1987, s. 49 i sled.

10 Cf. O. J u r e w i c z, *Historia literatury bizantyńskiej*, Wrocław 1984, p. 80-81.

11 S. R u n c i m a n, *The Byzantine Theocracy*, Cambridge University Pres, Cité d'après S. R u n c i m a n, *Teokracja bizantyńska*, Warszawa 1982, p. 27.

12 W. Ż i w o w, B. U s p i e n s k i j, op. cit., p. 142.

13 A. N. B e r d i a e v, *L'Idée russe*, Paris 1970, p. 42.

que dans "L'Apologie d'un fou" que Tchaadaev prend une attitude différente envers l'orthodoxie, en y voyant cette fois certains avantages, dont, d'après lui, le catholicisme était dépourvu.

En présentant la monarchie orthodoxe en tant que modèle idéal de l'Etat et du pouvoir, et par là glorifiant la Russie, Morozov juge sévèrement le modèle de l'Etat occidental. Il démontre les faiblesses et les dénaturations de celui-ci, de sorte que son exposé n'est plus seulement une apologie, mais devient aussi une critique.

Dans l'histoire de l'Europe occidentale, même si les symptômes du déclin étaient apparus bien avant, Morozov situe le tournant à l'époque de la Renaissance, qui, ajoutons-le au passage, n'a guère été présente en Russie. Le retour vers l'Antiquité proposé par la Renaissance, a fait, que l'on a commencé à abandonner les principes de la chrétienté, et après avoir quitté cette voie, le "nouveau monde s'est éloigné de la vérité beaucoup plus que ne l'avaient fait les Grecs et les Romains" (p. 11). P. Cet effondrement des cîmes auxquelles l'humanité s'était hissée grâce. à la chrétienté, devait entraîner des conséquences effroyables, proches de l'apostasie.

Morozov juge l'évolution de l'Europe Occidentale d'après des critères religieux et moraux. L'une des conséquences de ce regard tourné vers le monde antique a été un afflux de l'impiété et du mal. La liberté, celle qui était conforme aux idéaux chrétiens, s'est transformée en une liberté qui niait les principes éthiques fondamentaux. La nouvelle conception de la liberté a été fondée sur l'impiété et c'est ainsi que l'Europe Occidentale a en quelque sorte "dépassé" le monde antique, dans lequel les lois étaient créées sur des fondements religieux.

Une nouvelle structure de l'Etat commencait à émerger, structure qui a perturbé la hiérarchie des valeurs; les liens humains, familiaux et étatiques ont été remplacés par des liens artificiels fondés sur des contrats et des accords. Sont apparus alors les premiers symptômes d'une maladie, avec le plus puissant d'entre eux — la maladie révolutionnaire.

Dans la critique de la civilisation occidentale, Morozov met l'accent sur la révolution, qui d'après lui est le principal élément destructeur. En prenant une telle position, Morozov rejoint les déclarations des penseurs et des politiciens russes qui critiquaient la Révolution française, de même que les autres mouvements révolutionnaires, issue d'ailleurs de modes de penser et de systèmes philosophiques différents. Citons ici les noms de N. Karamzin, P. Tchaadaev et de N. Danilevski.

La révolution, d'après Morozov, comporte deux éléments destructeurs — les masses et les dictateurs, les empereurs. "Ces deux types de maladie révolutionnaire, écrit-il, affaiblissent l'Etat: la révolution mouvementée, par la souffrance et par l'élimination des bases de productivité et l'empire, quant à lui, par les guerres et les impôts" (p. 16). A cela s'ajoute un ébranlement de l'ordre juridique et le fonctionnement défectueux du système juridique. Cette altération touche la notion même du droit, et c'est alors qu'apparaît la formule "la loi est athée". Cette phrase devient l'expression de la volonté de la majorité des pécheurs et non plus l'incarnation de la volonté suprême, proclamée par l'Elu de Dieu. L'instabilité de la loi engendre la peur qui se transforme par la suite en terreur — "l'âme de la révolution", comme disait Marat.

Chez les fondamentalistes conservateurs orthodoxes, l'un des motifs quasiment obsessionnels, est la papauté. Il en est de même dans la critique de la civilisation occidentale proposée par Morozov. Selon lui, les papes en s'appropriant les attributs du pouvoir laïque trahissent le sens et l'essence même de la foi.

Selon Morozov, l'une des preuves de la maladie du christianisme est l'apparition du luthéranisme qu'il condamne pour d'autres raisons religieuses, à savoir l'élimination du sacerdoce et des ordinations (rukopoloženije — chirotonia). En détruisant l'unité du catholicisme, le protestantisme, au lieu de se tourner vers l'église orthodoxe, prônait le pouvoir illimité de la raison.

Au début, le catholicisme et le luthéranisme restaient en conflit pour arriver ensuite à une "sorte de paix en axant leurs efforts contre l'église orthodoxe. L'orient s'est rempli de missionnaires et de soi-disant maîtres". (p. 22)

La phobie anticatholique, d'ailleurs typiquement russe, est perceptible dans la caractéristique de l'ordre des Jésuites[14]. Rappelons ici que Catherine II, Paul Ier et Alexandre Ier ont été en principe favorables à cet ordre, restitué en 1814 par le pape Pie VII. En Russie, l'ordre des Jésuites se préoccupait essentiellement de l'enseignement, et à un degré inférieur de l'activité missionnaire (notamment en Crimée, en Sibérie, dans les régions d'Astrakhan et d'Orenbourg). Ils ont été aussi auprès des colonisateurs dans la région de la Volga où habitaient de nombreux catholiques. Cependant, l'activité des Jésuites a été comme nous l'avons dit, la plus importante dans le domaine de l'éducation. Le collège des Jésuites de Polock, avait obtenu en 1812 un statut d'école supérieure; un rôle important ont joué aussi les collèges et pensionnats de Petersbourg[15], d'Odessa et de Riga. M. Dovnar-Zapolski écrivait: "A Petersbourg les Jésuites ont fondé un institut que fréquentent les princes Yousoupor, Golitzyn, Orlov, Gagarin, Volkonski (...), certains d'entre eux sont devenus plus tard d'éminentes personnalistés de l'église catholique".[16] L'un des élèves du pensionnat jésuite, le prince P. Viazemski, soulignait dans ses mémoires, que "les Jésuites n'inculquaient jamais aux élèves l'idée de la supériorité du catholicisme sur l'église orthodoxe".[17]

---

14 L. Bazylow, *Społeczeństwo rosyjskie w pierwszej połowie XIX wieku*, Wrocław 1973, p. 312.

15 M. J. Rouet de Journel, *Un collège de Jésuits à Saint-Pétersbourg*, Paris 1922.

16 M. Downar-Zapolskij, *Idieały diekabristow*, Moskwa 1907, s. 38.

17 Połnoje sobranije soczinienij kn. P. A. Wiaziemskogo, T. I, Pietierburg 1878, s. XXIV.

En 1815, à la suite d'un décret, les Jésuites ont dû quitter immédiatement la ville de Petersbourg et il leur a été défendu de séjourner dans la "vieille capitale" Moscou. Après quelques années, en 1820, le ministre de l'Education, A. Golitayn, présenta au tsar un mémorial dans lequel il était dit, que les jésuites étaient bel et bien chassés de l'Empire russe et qu'ils ne pourraient y revenir dans l'avenir.

Cette attitude hostile envers les Jésuites s'est manifestée aussi par le fait de leur attribuer "l'intrigue" visant à rendre impossible la réorganisation de l'église catholique romaine en Russie. Le projet d'une telle réorganisation avait été proposé par un rénégat polonais S. Siestrzeńcewicz, qui voulait soumettre l'église catholique au pouvoir de l'Etat d'après le modèle établi entre l'église orthodoxe et l'Etat. M. Morochkine, auteur de l'ouvrage "Les Jésuites en Russie" écrivait: "Ainsi, l'intrigue jésuite a fait échouer pour toujours l'un des projets les plus salutaires pour la paix en Russie et pour tous ceux qui appartiennent à la foi latine".[18]

Comme le constate L. Bazylow, "l'ouvrage volumineux de Morochkine, est l'exemple d'un alliage rarissime d'obscurantisme, de chauvinisme et de bêtise. L'auteur est submergé par la haine non seulement envers les Jésuites, mais envers le catholicisme et la polonité".[19] Une attitude semblable envers les Jésuites est présente chez de nombreux publicistes, et notamment chez Morozov, qui constate, que "l'ordre des Jésuites nuisait à la Russie à un degré aussi important que les associations"(p. 37), et plus loin: "l'ordre des Jésuites tente d'influencer certaines personnalités éminentes, les femmes, sachant que c'est par leur intermédiare que l'avilissement passera dans les masses populaires". (p. 37)

L'un des points sur lesquels la critique de Morozov devient particulièrement violente est le "libéralisme", qu'il appelle "faux libéralisme" (lżeliberalizm). Dans la perspective adoptée par Morozov, une telle appellation est tout-à-fait logique, comme cela est d'ailleurs le cas d'une autre formule — "la maladie libérale".

Par "faux libéralisme", Morozov entend l'ensemble des phénomènes da la socio-politique et de la réflexion philosophique, socio-politique et religieuse qui ne sont pas conformes au modèle de l'état idéal, c'est-à-dire à la monarchie orthodoxe, forme qui est celle de la Russie. L'auteur distingue deux éléments: d'une part l'élément natif, dont les sources remontent au système de rassemblements de Novgorod, aux temps des troubles ("smuta"), à l'anarchie cosaque,

---

[18] M. M o r o s z k i n, *Iezuity w Rossii s carstwowanija Jekatieriny II i do naszego wriemieni*, T. II. Pietierburg 1870, s. 252.

[19] L. B a z y l o w, op. cit., p. 313.

et de l'autre, l'élément venu de l'étranger, qui date de l'époque de Pierre Ier. Ce dernier élément est encore divisé en deux catégories: catholique-romaine et protestante. Leur influence a eu pour effet la formation d'organisations maçonniques des rose-croix (influence du catholicisme et des Jésuites), et l'apparition des illuministes (influence du protestantisme). L'Apparition de nombreuses sectes (doukhobortsy, klysty, doukhonostsy, skoptsy), Morozov attribue à la présence de ce "faux libéralisme". Selon Morozov, des conséquences néfastes ont été entrainées par l'intérêt excessif porté à la langue française, ce qui a déclenché l'épidémie de la libre pensée, dès le règne de Catherine II. Des adeptes du "faux libéralisme", comme N. Novikov ou Lopuchin ont propagé des écrits quasi-religieux, contraires à l'othodoxie et à la moralité. L'influence de la pensée occidentale, et notamment celle des oeuvres de Voltaire, a été alors possible à cause d'une censure défaillante qui a facilité une "propagande nuisible".[20]

Dans le domaine religieux, le "faux libéralisme" s'est amplifié lors du règne d'Alexandre Ier. De nombreux ouvrages soi-disant religieux (J. Gassner, H. Stilling, J. Krüdener) ont été publiés à cette époque. "Tous ces ouvrages, écrit Morozov, ont popularisé les dénaturations de l'église catholique romaine et du protestantisme". (p. 43)

Pour Morozov, l'une des idées fausses qui vient de l'Occident est l'idée de l'égalité — "produit de l'aveuglement de l'esprit et de l'obscurantisme spirituel" (p. 36). Au communisme et au faux libéralisme Morozov oppose le libéralisme chrétien, qui étant basé sur l'amour, permet une coexistence des classes supérieures et inférieures.

Après cette constatation on comprend mieux l'attitude hostile de Morozov envers les droits de l'homme, proclamés par l'Assemblé Nationale française, d'autant plus, comme il le souligne, que l'on n'y trouvait pas la liste des devoirs.

La France de la Révolution et de la Commune de Paris représente aux yeux de Morozov le lieu des actes instigateurs et des événements que les Bourbons n'ont pas reussi à maîtriser. Il s'adonne à une critique tout aussi bien du système républicain ("la fièvre républicaine") qu'à celui du despotisme ("les frissons despotiques"). "Un cas grave, écrit-il, s'est transformé en un cas chronique, permanent: la France est atteinte d'une maladie mortelle". Morozov prend aussi une attitude hostile et sans équivoque contre Napoléon III et sa politique étrangère. L'idée réalisée par ce monarque, selon Morozov, comporte

---

20 A noter l'attitude hostile envers les Jésuits d'un certain nombre de Russes progressistes, d'esprits éclairés, comme par exemple V. Pečerin. Voir: L. S u c h a n e k, *Les catholiques russes et les procatholiques en Russia dans la première moitié du XIXe siècle*, Cahiers du Monde russe et soviétique, XXIX (3-4), juillet-décembre. 1988, p. 365.

"la folie la plus meurtière qui ait été créée dans l'histoire du monde" (p. 24).Elle est le synonyme d'une guerre incessante et globale, politique et religieuse, qui englobe les conflits et la discorde entre les nations et les gouvernements.

Morozov procède à l'opposition de deux idées prédominantes à cette époque: l'idée napoléonienne et l'idée orthodoxe. La première d'entre elles représente la déstabilisation de la vie, la déchéance des valeurs éternelles, la remise en question de la hiérarchie de l'ordre des valeurs. L'idée orthodoxe en est l'opposition pure. E. Cioran constate, à juste titre, que "chaque civilisation estime non seulement avoir le mode de vie juste, mais aussi que son rôle consiste à convertir à ce mode tous les autres".[21]

Comme d'autres penseurs, idéologues et publicistes russes[22], Morozov proclame l'idée d'une mission que la Russie se doit de remplir: "Ce qui attend la Russie, c'est l'acte de sauver le monde" (p. 27). Il écrit: "L'Europe ne peut subsister sous la forme actuelle(...). Elle doit devenir russe ou libérale (c'est-à-dire périr aprés une révolution)"(p. 45)

Le salut de l'Europe ne pourra pas être l'oeuvre de la Prusse, de l'Autriche, de la France ou de l'Angleterre. Ce salut ne peut venir que de la Russie. "En Russie, écrit avec orgueil Morozov, brille le soleil de l'Orthodoxie, et c'est vers cette lumière que se retourneront tous les peuples"(p. 46). Cet élément de la théorie de Morozov se situe dans le courant de la pensée russe du XIX138[me] siècle, et notamment dans la réflexion sur la philosophie de l'histoire. Berdiaev constate: "sur les fondements de la philosophie de l'histoire s'est formée notre conscience nationale. Et ce n'est pas par hasard qu'au centre de nos préoccupations spirituelles se retrouvent les querelles entre les slavophiles et les occidentalistes, sur la Russie et l'Europe, sur l'Orient et l'Occident".[23] Chez Morozov toutefois, la conception philosophique est intimement liée à l'idée politique du grand empire et est l'expression de la politique impériale.

Dans le texte de Morozov apparaît souvent le motif panslaviste. Le salut de l'Europe restera en rapport avec la création d'un empire chrétien, dont la capitale sera la Reine des Villes — Constantinople, libérée des mains des musulmans. De la Sainte Sofia (Hagia Sophia), viendra la sagesse divine qui illuminera l'occident et le sauvera de la foile. Mais si l'Europe occidentale rejette cette aide, elle s'effondrera, accablée par des agitations constantes, par la misère et la famine causées par la destruction des forces productives.

---

21 E. C i o r a n, *Histoire et utopie*, Gallimard, Paris 1960, p. 33-52, Traduction polonaise *Rosja i wirus wolności*, Zeszyty Literackie, 1985, Nr 9, p. 78-87.

22 Voir L. S u c h a n e k, *Pierre Tchaadaev sur la mission de la Russie* In: Messianisme et slavophilie, Cracovie 1987, p. 173-179.

23 N. B i e r d i a j e w, *Smysł istorii*, Wtoroje izd. Paris 1969.

De nombreux Russes pensaient à un état idéal; dont l'incarnation serait justement la Russie. On a beaucoup écrit sur le côté spécifique culturel et historique de ce pays. Cette thèse a été par exemple présentée par Danilevski, auteur de l'ouvrage "La Russie et l'Europe". De même, Leontiev dans son travail sur Byzance et les Slaves considérait la Russie comme un pays différent sur le plan de la civilisation par rapport aux autres pays de l'Europe.

La pensée de Morozov qui unit des éléments d'historicisme aux mots d'ordre politiques de l'époque, permet de mieux comprendre la mentalité et l'esprit d'une partie de la société russe. Ce groupe rejetait l'ouverture à l'occidentalisme en associant l'isolationnisme culturel et civilisationnel à des penchants impérialistes.

L'un des reflets de la conception de Morozov que nous avons présentée ici, et même s'il est difficile d'établir des preuves de similitudes génétiques, est la réflexion de G. Šimanov. Nous ne pouvons parler dans ce cas que d'une parenté typologique. Dans ce texte publié dans les éditions clandestines — Moscou — Rome III, il écrit, que l'idée d'une théocratie orthodoxe future est la seule idée créative existante de nos jours.[24] Après Octobre, selon Šimanov, devrait maintenant survenir une orthodoxisation du monde entier.

Dans un autre, Šimanov constatait, que le pouvoir soviétique reste imprégné de théocratie et si dans l'avenir le parti communiste se transforme en Parti Orthodoxe d'Union Soviétique, c'est alors qu'apparaîtra l'Etat idéal.[25]

---

24 G. S z i m a n o w, *Moskwa — Trietij Rim*, Moskowskij Almanach, 1974, 7 ijul.

25 G. S z i m a n o w, *Idiealnoje gosudarstwo*, Moskowskij Almanach, 1975, 29 maja; Voir à son sujet: A. J a n o w, *Państwo idealne Gennadija Szymanowa*, Aneks, 1979, Nr 22, p. 95-111.

Anna Raźny — Université Jagellonne, Cracovie

Vladimir Boukovski — la lutte avec l'Occident pour l'Occident

Vladimir Boukovski, militant pour la démocratie et les droits de l'homme en Union Soviétique, dissident, prisonnier politique, plusieurs fois condamné au camp de travail et hôpitaux psychiatriques, obligé à èmigrer, et enfin écrivain et publiciste, est connu avant tout grâce à son livre *Et le vent reprend ses tours...*

Son livre c'est une autobiographie d'un militant, prisonnier, patient des hôpitaux psychiatriques, une chronique des événements les plus importants qui ont eu lieu en URSS depuis la deuxième guerre mondiale jusqu'à 1976, l'année où l'auteur a dû quitter le pays pour émigrer à l'Occident. Ce livre c'est aussi un traité sociopolitique et moral dans lequel Boukovski fait la critique sévère du système soviétique. Dans l'autobiographie ainsi que dans le traité l'auteur consacre beaucoup de pages au sujet de l'Occident.

La trame autobiographique y est liée à la problématique sociopolitique et morale. L'enfance et la jeunesse de Boukovski nous montre l'histoire de la génération d'après-guerre. C'est cette génération-là qui mûrit pour entreprendre vers la fin des années 60 l'action au profit des droits de l'homme et la démocratisation en Union Soviétique.

Le souci principal de l'auteur est d'écrire l'épanouissement autonome de la conscience de l'homme inscrit dans le système qui lui est hostile et qui le soumet à l'action destructive. L'épanouissement autonome et individuel de la conscience constitue non seulement la base de l'action, mais aussi la garantie de la libération intérieure qui permet à l'homme de rompre les fers du système.

Le développement de la conscience est determiné par la découverte de la vérité, dissimulée par les idéologues et politiques. La vérité sur le système soviétique et sur l'homme qui y est condamné à vivre est liée à la découverte de l'Occident et la vérité sur cette Europe-là.

L'image du système soviétique présentée dans le livre de Boukovski ainsi que l'image de l'Occident n'ont point de caractère d'abstrait spéculatif, détaché de la réalité quotidienne et de la dimension historique.

L'expérience intérieure et spirituelle de l'auteur qui est aussi celle historique de sa génération décide de l'authenticité de l'image faite par Boukovski. Cette image est liée avec la collectivité (ici la société soviétique) au nom de laquelle le dissident s'engage dans son action.

Le sort individuel et celui de la génération est étroitement lié au sort de la collectivité. Dans les deux cas l'attitude à l'égard de l'Occident joue un grand rôle. Elle résulte de la politique officielle de l'Occident vis-à-vis de l'URSS ainsi que les rapports inofficiels concernant le sort des citoyens soviétiques.

L'attitude de Boukovski à l'égard de l'Occident est floue. Elle change avec le temps. La même est l'attitude de toute la génération des dissidents et de la majorité de la société qui ne s'identifie pas avec le système soviétique. Cette instabilité des opinions sur l'Occident dépend de la réaction de celui-ci sur le système soviétique. Ces opinions dépendent surtout du niveau de la conscience historique, socio-politique et axiologique (ici morale) du dissident-militant ainsi que de la collectivité.

Dans ces deux types de conscience l'histoire officielle et celle inofficielle (privée) sont toujours antagonistes. Tout ce qui est inofficiel, dans la dimension individuelle et collective, signifie toujours ce qui est absolument différent de ce qui est officiel. Cela apparaît aussi dans l'image de l'Occident faite par Russes.

L'image officielle de l'Occident accompagne le citoyen soviétique dès la petite enfance jusqu'à la grande vieillesse; dès l'école maternelle jusqu'à l'âge de la retraite. En Union Soviétique, dans l'image officielle des années 50, 60, l'Occident c'est la misère, le chômage, la pourriture morale et la source de l'impérialisme; la menace pour la paix. Cette image est propagée partout — dans les écoles, universités et entreprises. Elle est popularisée dans les média, toutes les formes de culture et de sciences. Cette image est donc toujours à l'opposé de l'Union Soviétique. L'URSS c'est le synonyme du socialisme, donc du progrès, de la justice, du bon travail et de la garantie de la paix. L'Occident — synonyme le capitalisme, c'est à dire l'injustice, l'obscurantisme, le chômage et la menace de la guerre.

Le plus typique est dans ce cas-là l'émission des actualités qu'on passe avant les films. L'image y faite présente le mal qui naît du capitalisme (la misère, le chômage etc.) ainsi que le mal qui ne dépend pas du système socio-politique: les catastrophes, les fléaux et les cataclysmes.

En URSS, c'est à dire dans le système idéal socio-politique, il n'existe pas la misère, le chômage et la dépravation morale, il n'y a pas non plus de cataclysmes et de fléaux. Dans l'image officielle l'opposition l'URSS — l'Occident concerne les idées, la politique, la culture et même la nature et le cosmos.

Dans cette opposition Boukovski souligne surtout l'aspect de l'idée et de la politique et néglige tous les problèmes qui se rapportent à la métaphysique et la réligion.Ce qui l'intéresse au niveau de l'idée et de la politique ce sont les problèmes de la démocratie et de la liberté qui en découlent. Pour Boukovski la démocratie est la garantie de la liberté. Elle facilite les choix socio-politiques ainsi que ceux axiologiques. La démocratie favorise la connaissance de la vérité et ouvre l'esprit de l'homme aux valeurs absolues. Ce point de vue, dès le début du livre, permet de situer l'auteur dans le mouvement oppositionnel qui est démocratique et anti-totalitaire. Ce mouvement — ci rejette l'idée du socialisme parce qu'il ne croit pas à son amélioration et la possibilité de le réformer.

Cette attitude sera confirmée par son engagement du dissident. Dans son livre il souligne que ce mouvement oppositionnel qu'il représente n'a rien à voir avec le néo-marxisme, les dissidents marxistes et la gauche libérale. Dans son attitude il est loin aussi de l'orientation chrétienne et nationale, mais il ne lui est pas hostile.

La critique de l'image officielle de l'Occident et le jugement inofficiel, individuel de l'auteur, présentés dans son livre, résultent de son attitude. En nous présentant son histoire de mûrir dans l'esprit et de découvrir la vérité Boukovski souligne que, déjà à l'école, il a éprouvé ce qu'il appelle l'illumination.

Cette illumination arrive tôt ou un peu plus tard à chacun des citoyens soviétiques qui ne s'indentifie pas avec le système. Elle consiste à découvrir que tout ce qui est officiel n'est pas vrai; et cette découverte est subite et inattendue. La volonté de découvrir la vérité et de démasquer le mensonge en sera la conséquence. La vérité touche l'Europe. Grâce aux divers contacts avec l'Occident (surtout par la presse et la radio) on peut apprendre que dans son système on ne meurt pas de faim et de misère, les magasins sont pleins de marchsandises, on n'y fait pas la queue et les chômeurs reçoivent des allocations chômage pour vivre. Et il devient de plus en plus évident que le socialisme ne fait pas s'approcher les gens de l'avenir rêvé, mais au contraire, il les en fait éloigner. En plus, il devient de plus en plus clair que le socialisme est fondé sur le mensonge, l'exploitation et la contrainte. Il devient de plus en plus clair que la société soviétique est malade: elle est passive et immorale, infectée par la corruption. Il y a beaucoup de types de corruption, mais elle se rapporte toujours aux relations entre le citoyen et le gouvernement. L'amoralisme du citoyen est officiel, soviétique. Dans la privée, comme souligne Constantin Simis dans son livre La société corrompue[1], le citoyen soviétique agira conformément aux préceptes généraux de l'éthique humaine.

---

1 C. S i m i s, *La société corrompue*, Ed. Robert Laffont, Paris 1983.

Dans ses relations avec le gouvernement il se sert de la corruption "spontanément et machinalement, pour obtenir ce dont il a besoin — et c'est généralement un besoin vital". Et, parlant de la corruption, Simis continue:

"Il mentira à un représentant du gouvernement, mais sera sincère et honnête dans ses relations avec ses amis et voisins; il volera avec joie vingt paquets de cigarettes à la manufacutre de tabac où il travaille, mais ne dérobera pas un centime à autrui.

Cette double morale s'explique par la profonde désaffection que le peuple soviétique éprouve pour son gouvernement. Le citoyen soviétique discerne rarement le caractère totalitaire du régime, il reconnaît rarement les relations négatives qu'il entretient avec lui. Il répond instinctivement aux privations matérielles, au manque de liberté, à la corruption totale de ceux qui le gouvernent, à l'immoralité du régime, en excluant de sa sphère de valeurs morales tout ce qui a trait à l'Etat et l'économie de l'Etat".[2]

Boukovski dit que la découverte de la vérité signifie le changement dans l'opposition: l'Occident — l'Union Soviétique. Ce changement a le caractère axiologique. Il se situe dans ce que Thomas Stearne Eliot appelle l'espace prépolitique.

Cet espace c'est l'espace des valeurs qui permettent à l'homme de vivre selon sa condition humaine.

L'Occident présenté officiellement, sous un faux jour, devient positif. L'image du système soviétique va de paire avec le vif intérêt pour l'Occident. Cet intérêt est naturel. Il n'est pas inspirier par ce qui constitue la dimension stable de l'existence de l'homme. Il signifie le besoin de posséder les valeurs fondamentales ainsi que l'envie de participer dans l'ordre de ses valeurs.

Dans la conscience de Boukovski — dissident et militant apparaît une norme axiologique qui permet d'une façon autonome apprécier et juger l'opposition entre l'Occident et l'Union Soviétique. Cette norme naît du christianisme et de l'humanisme européen (qui selon certains savants constitue une forme secularisée du christianisme).

Cette norme est accompagnée du désir de vaincre ce qui porte atteinte aux valeurs fondamentales. Ce désir est lié avec les mythes de vaincre (surmonter) le mal, les mythes qui, eux aussi, ont formé l'identité des nations européennes.

La norme spirituelle et éthique dirige Boukovski vers l'Occident. Dans sa conscience de dissident l'Occident vit sa grande tradition européenne. L'at-

---

2 Op. cit., p. 250.

titude de Boukovski envers l'Europe occidentale permet de le mettre au nombre des occidentalistes russes du XIX s.

Pendant que ceux-ci s'inspirent des utopies, des hérésies politiques et des pensées relativistes issues de la Révolution Française, Boukovski fait appel aux valeurs absolues dans la tradition européenne, aux valeurs qui déterminent l'existence de l'individu et de la société. Sa lutte avec le système devient en même temps la lutte avec les idéologies totalitaires et le relativisme des valeurs conçues à l'Occident et réalisées en définitive par les révolutionnaires et communistes russes.

Boukovski se demande jusqu'à quel point les doctrines venues de L'Occident sont applicables en Russie. Dans le système soviétique il reconnaît des éléments occidentalistes. La seule doctrine politique que Boukovski, comme Dostoïevski, condamne absolument et honnit, c'est le socialisme, celui de l'Internationale et de la Commune de Paris, celui du Palais de Cristal comme celui de la fourmillière.

Cette image inofficielle, individuelle de l'Occident commune pour une génération de dissidents russes est le contraire de l'URSS. Mais ce qui diffère les deux oppositions a le caractère moins socio-politique, mais plutôt axiologique. Le rôle principal joue ici la catégorie du mal qui passe du côté de l'Union Soviétique.

Cette image inofficielle et claire jusqu'à présent subit une déformation quand Boukovski dans son activité du dissident compte sur l'aide occidentale. Il vient assez vite à la conclusion que l'Occident n'est pas donc unanime à réagir au mal. Les communistes et la gauche intellectuelle des années 60 et 70 ne soutiennent pas le mouvement de dissidents, ne s'engagent pas à la critique authentique du système soviétique. Ils parlent d'eurocommunisme et du socialisme "au visage humain", ce qui nous montre qu'ils acceptent l'idée du socialisme comme digne de programmer et d'être réalisée.

Cependant pour Boukovski l'idée du socialisme "au visage humain" est aussi à rejeter de même que l'idée du fascisme "au visage humain". Les communistes et la gauche intellectuelle déforment l'image de l'Union Soviétique. Ils ne disent pas la vérité sur la réalité, ce qui fait désorienter l'opinion publique à l'Occident. Ils ne montrent pas non seulement les points négatifs du système, mais ils ne disent pas non plus la vérité sur le mouvement dissident. Ils le montrent comme le révisionnisme, la manifestation du néomarxisme. Boukovski critique leur naïveté d'idées, leur partialité idéoloqique ainsi que leurs opinions superficielles et fausses sur la réalité soviétique. Il corrige leurs déclarations surtout celles qui concernent le mouvement dissident. Il souligne que les révisionnistes et les marxistes y étaient isolés et peu nombreux. Les communistes et la gauche n'influencent pas très fort l'opinion publique de l'Occident. Le rôle principal de former l'opinion appartient aux média, à la littérature et au film. Le grand rôle y est joué par les journalistes, les publicistes et éditeurs qui négligent les opinions stéréotypées sur l'URSS et essaient de découvrir la vérité. Et c'est sur les pages de son livre que Boukovski rend hommage à ceux d'entre eux qui malgré les difficultés et les répressions du côté des autorités soviétiques entraient en contact avec les dissidents. C'étaient eux qui transmettaient l'information vraie et l'appel de venir en aide à la société soviétique.

Il remarque quand même que certains des correspondants occidentaux sont encore paralysés par la même peur qui paralysait l'Occident à l'époque stalinienne. Cette peur-là ne permet pas de parler des répressions, de misère et de contrainte.

De cette peur dépendent aussi des institutions et des sociétés scientifiques (psychiatriques entre autre) auxquelles des dissidents s'adressent. Il les accuse d'être opportunistes et hypocrites. Pour la même raison il accuse aussi les gens politiques, les idéologues de l'Occident et même l'ONU. Il les critique de garder le silence en 1968 pendant l'invasion de Prague.

— "Ils préféraient discuter de Rodésie..." —

Leur silence signifiait l'acceptation et la coparticipation muette à l'invasion. C'était aussi l'acceptation de la violence et la trahison des grandes valeurs de la tradition européenne. Les opinions occidentales sur le système communiste et ses manifestations de contrainte, de force et d'impérialisme, expriment le rapport de l'Occident à son identité spirituelle et éthique.

Ici l'Occident n'est pas uniforme. Dans ses sociétés il y a des gens qui gardent cette identité ou s'en éloignent. Les élites du pouvoir se conduisent toujours de la même façon — ils nient l'identité européenne spirituelle et éthique. Ce comportement fait que l'opposition l'Occident — l'URSS disparaît au niveau axiologique. Le mal apparaît de deux côtés. De deux cotés on nie la vérité. Et comme l'a écrit Hannah Arendt: "La vérité, quoique sans pouvoir et toujours défaite quand elle se heurte de front avec les pouvoirs en place quels qu'ils soient, possède une force propre: quoi que puissent combiner ceux qui sont au pouvoir, ils sont incapables d'en découvrir ou inventer un substitut viable. La persuasion et la violence peuvent détruire la vérité, mais ils ne peuvent la remplacer".[3]

Mais l'Occident ne veut rien savoir. Les notions telles que la justice, le bien, les droits de l'homme y sont relativisées; elles ne se rapportent à aucune réalité supérieure et absolue. On peut les employer librement et les utiliser dans les fins différentes.

---

[3] H. A r e n d t, *La crise de la culture*, Gallimard 1989, p. 330.

Boukovski exprime aussi un tel jugement sur l'Occident dans son journalisme et dans sa brochure "Les pacifistes contre la paix". Il y dévoile la soumission de l'Occident à l'impérialisme soviétique ce qui signifie l'éloignement des traditions spirituelles de l'Europe. Boukovski met l'accent ici sur la menace pour le mouvement dissident en URSS et pour l'Occident lui-même. L'abandon des traditions et de l'identité le rend impuissant et désarmé devant le mal totalitaire.

Cela témoigne de la crise profonde de l'Occident. L'Occident a décidé de ne plus penser au mal. "Décrétant la fin des idéologies, il neutralisait silencieusement les problèmes éthiques et édifiait son nouveau monde en deçà (dans l'économie politique) du bien et du mal ou par-delà (dans la futurologie d'un équilibre purement technique des armements, de la coexistence promise pacifique, de l'Europe réconciliée de l'Atlantique à l'Oural des camps)".[4]

Le retour à la norme spirituelle et éthique y sera une solution pour l'Europe. Et la lutte avec le mal en fera la preuve. Dans la critique de l'Occident Boukovski lutte pour l'Occident. Il veut l'épargner du mal qui s'est enraciné dans le système soviétique. Mais l'Occident doit vouloir y faire face.

"La violence — écrit Boukovski vers la fin du livre *Et le vent reprend ses tours...*" — se venge impitoyablement de ceux qui la favorisent. Et ceux qui croient que la ligne entre l'esclavage et la liberté tombe là où tombent les frontières de l'Union Soviétique, se trompent énormément" (tr. A. R.).[5]

---

4 A. Glucksman, *La force du vertige*, Paris 1983, p. 134.

5 W. Bukowski, *I powraca wiatr...*, Polonia, Paryż 1985.

Maria Cieśla-Korytowska — Université Jagellonne, Cracovie

Mickiewicz et les Slaves: que peuvent-ils offrir à l'Occident?

Lorsqu'on lit aujourd'hui la "Littérature slave" de Mickiewicz, on a l'impression que les idées du poète-professeur sont plutôt dépassées et qu'en même temps elles nous sont très proches. Il serait donc peut-être intéressant de voir pourquoi il en est ainsi. Est-ce que, parmi les idées les plus générales de Mickiewicz, celles qui concernent l'essence de la nation et les relations réciproques entre elles, ou même ses opinions historiques, ne méritent pas un moment de réflexion ou de polémique? Est-ce que même ses visions idéalisées et optimistes de l'avenir possible doivent nous être étrangères?[1]

Dans les cours de Mickiewicz, présentés au Collège de France, on trouve plusieurs problèmes importants, dont la solution acceptée par le poète mérite, semble-t-il, notre réflexion. C'est, en premier lieu, la question de l'identité et de la particularité des nations. La deuxième question, en quelque sorte opposée à la première, est celle de la communauté des nations. Enfin, en troisième lieu, vient la question des quelques conclusions concrètes de Mickiewicz concernant la nation, la civilisation et la politique. L'actualité de ces problèmes semble évidente pour tout le monde. Les réflexions de Mickiewicz qui nous intéressent ici se concentrent autour des quatre thèmes suivants: 1. l'unité ou le dispersement des Slaves, 2. leur spécifité par rapport aux autres nations, 3. leurs relations avec l'Europe Occidentale, 4. la place et le rôle des Polonais.

L'unité des Slaves

Lorsque Mickiewicz essaye de présenter les Slaves à l'Europe Occidentale, il veut d'une part les montrer en opposition avec l'Occident (comme une entité historique et culturelle), mais de l'autre il est conscient qu'ils ne sont pas homogènes. D'après lui on ne peut parler de l'unité des Slaves que par rapport

---

1 Je vais, bien évidemment, faire abstraction des opinions concrètes et du savoir de Mickiewicz qui certainement diffèrent des nôtres et qui ont différé parfois aussi de ceux de ses contemporains. Il est également évident que la langue ainsi que certaines conceptions philosophiques propres au romantisme doivent être traitées aujourd'hui avec une certaine distance.

à un passé lointain, légendaire, ainsi qu'à un futur rêvé. Aux temps historiques la communauté slave n'existe pas. Les causes en sont diverses, dit Mickiewicz. C'est le fait d'avoir accepté le christianisme de deux sources différentes et, par suite, d'avoir créé deux traditions différentes dans les relations Etat-Eglise (pouvoir séculaire — pouvoir ecclésiastique), qui en est une des plus essentielles.

La manière dont le christianisme a été introduit par les souverains — sans conflits entre les Polonais ("Lachs") et les tchèques ("Czechs"), par force en Russie normande — est une des différences les plus importantes. C'est ainsi que s'est faite la division des Slaves en Polonais et Tchèques d'un côté[2] et en Russes de l'autre. Ces derniers se sont approprié dès le début de l'historie une tradition normande, étrangère aux Slaves: la tradition de gouverner. Les Tchèques ont ensuite abandonné, eux aussi, la tradition primitive et ils sont entrés dans l'orbite du système allemand. Mickiewicz nous laisse deviner que seuls les Polonais n'ont pas souillé la tradition primordiale, dont la République nobiliaire, basée sur la libre élection, était une simple continuation. D'après lui, même si la légende des trois frères, Lech, Czech et Rus, exprime une vérité historique, elle parle d'un temps et de traditions oubliés par les Slaves: "Cette unité n'a jamais existé. L'unité des peuples ne se trouve écrite que sur la première page de la Bible; elle se retrouvera, nous l'espérons, sur la dernière page de la vraie philosophie. Avant l'historie politique, aucun lien général ne reliait les Slaves entre eux; cette historie elle-même n'a constamment travaillé qu'à détruire des caractères communs dont il n'existe persque plus de traces aujourd'hui(...). Les savants invoquent toujours la communauté de race, oubliant que ce sont les institutions religieuses et politiques qui ont créé les séparations qu'ils voudraient anéantir, et qu'il est impossible de détruire tout le passé historique d'une nation pour la ramener à son origine physique".[3] Ainsi donc Mickiewicz distingue nettement les temps préhistoriques, légendaires et les temps historiques. Le démembrement actuel — politique, culturel, spirituel — résulte des conditions, ou plutôt des décisions historiques, qui ont formé des nations slaves particulières en accord avec leur tradi-tion mythique — ou bien contre elle.

Où se trouve donc, selon Mickiewicz (tout inconséquent qu'il est à ce propos), l'unité ou plutôt la spécifité des Slaves; où voit-il une caractéristique qui leur permette de se distinguer des autres nations? Car

---

2 Mickiewicz souligne le fait que les Tchèques et les Polonais ont eu assez longtemps un type de système politique semblable, des rois de la même famille, une histoire commune.

3 La traduction des fragments de la "Littérature slave" provient de l'auteur de l'article.

plusieurs fois il nomme certains phénomènes ou époques historiques "slaves" ou "non-slaves". En voici des exemples. L'époque de Stanislas August en Pologne a été non-slave, non-nationale — et cela pour trois raisons: 1. le Ier partage de la Pologne a eu lieu à cette époque-là, 2. même la confédération de Bar, profondément "slave d'esprit" (car prenant pour mot d'ordre la l i b e r t é et la f o i) en est venue à rompre avec la tradition de la non-violence (l'attentat contre le roi), 3. la culture et la littérature ont commencé à se développer rapidement, mais elles acceptaient des exemples étrangers à notre tradition, issus de la raison éclairée (Trembecki, la satire comme genre littéraire etc.).

Ce qui est donc non-slave par excellence, c'est la violence, contraire à la tradition de la liberté et de la foi, qui prend pour objectif la personne du roi et la nation. De même l'époque de Pierre Ier, tsar de Russie, sera "non-slave", car fondée sur la tyrannie et sur des modèles étrangers (prussiens). La r a i s o n, l' e s p r i t (dans le sens "avoir de l'esprit"), sont un autre trait "non-slave", étranger à la spiritualité slave.

Mickiewicz voit donc l'unité possible des Slaves dans leur trait commun qu'il cherche dans le domaine de ce que nous appelerions aujourd'hui mentalité; il l'oppose à la raison. Il part de la notion de "duch", parole intraduisible d'après lui, mais présente dans toutes les langues slaves. La spécifité culturelle des Slaves est fondée justement sur cette notion. Mickiewicz s'étend sur elle et sur l'impossibilité de la traduire. Ce n'est ni "mens" ni "âme", mais l'esprit dans le sens du revenant (voir un esprit), aussi bien que du génie, "l'homme spirituel", l'homme intime qui anime le corps, le s p i r i t u s au sens biblique (11.II.1842). Ce "spiritualisme" des Slaves est, d'après Mickiewicz, un des traits immanents du caractère, du tempérament et de l'esprit des Slaves qui les distingue des autres peuples d'Europe. Il est un déterminant décisif de leur culture et de leur vocation future. Le poète en parle dans la parabole du navire, où il se sert de la métaphore de la vapeur — force motrice que certaines nations ont utilisée pour de grandes oeuvres de civilisation matérielle (Egypte) ou spirituelle, ou bien pour s'assurer le confort et le luxe (gentil manque d'exemples). Les Slaves l'ont gardée pure croit Mickiewicz et n'ont pas encore décidé de son usage.

Tout en constatant que les Slaves possèdent en commun le caractère spirituel, le poète ne manque pas de remarquer les différences dans ce qu'il appelle — dans son language messiano-towianiste — le "ton" des nations slaves particulières. Les Tchèques ont donc développé surtout cet organe d'esprit qui s'appelle la raison (développement des sciences); les Russes, n'ayant pas pu développer le leur se sont assimilé (sous l'influence des Huns et des Normands) le "ton mongol", ton de violence et de contrainte. Les Polonais ont développé le ton chrétien, pareil à celui qui animait la France au Moyen Age.

Cet "esprit" ou "ton" se manifeste dans les différents domaines de la vie. Mickiewicz parle surtout de l'histoire, de la politique et de la littérature qui est pour lui l'élément le plus important de la culture. De même donc qu'il juge dangereux d'emprunter des types de système politique aux autres nations il croit nocif d'appliquer aveuglément leurs exemples littéraires — tout excellents qu'ils soient (Walter Scott). Continuer sa propre tradition avec la conscience de sa particularité, voilà le chemin juste du développement national.

Les Slaves et l'Occident

Pourrait-on alors, d'après ce qui vient d'être dit, parler de xénophobie ou même de nationalisme ou de chauvinisme? Il semble que non. La plus grande valeur, décisive pour la cohérence de l'Europe, est, pour Mickiewicz, le christianisme. Cette opinion va revenir dans tous ses cours pour atteindre son apogée dans le messianisme. Dans le Ier cours du Ier cycle Mickiewicz parle déjà de l'Europe (il emploie cette notoin alternativement avec celle de l'Occident), dont la France est le centre. C'est elle, "la fille aînée de l'Eglise", qui réalise le dogme chrétien de l'union des nations. Le poète parle aussi du penchant éternel des Slaves vers l'Europe et du refus de celle-ci de les accepter en tant que membres de la "société chrétienne", de l'Occident autrement dit. Mickiewicz voit un des buts de ses cours dans la tentative d'aider ses compatriotes à s'approcher de l'Europe ou bien d'aider l'Europe à les accepter. Il est le plus facile d'accepter en connaissant justement la culture, et notamment la littérature; on se rend compte alors que toute oeuvre européene provient de la même source. On pourrait, à ce propos, reconnaître en Mickiewicz le saint patron de tous ces poètes-philosophes-professeurs polonais qui poursuivent sa tâche jusqu' à nos jours.

Il est en même temps significatif que Mickiewicz n'essaie pas d'insister à tout prix sur les r e s s e m b l a n c e s entre l'Ouest et le Nord (qu'on appelle maintenant l'Est). Bien au contraire, il accentue surtout les différences culturelles et il cherche la valeur dans le particulier et le divers. Quand il parle des ressemblances, il ne le fait que dans le but "méthodologique" (pour approcher et rendre plus facile à comprendre).[4] Il agit de la même façon lorsqu'il compare les oeuvres littéraires analogues (l'épopée médiévale, p.ex. "La Chanson de

---

4 Mickiewicz parle p. ex. des ressemblances entre les Slaves balcaniques et les Espagnols, entre les Tchèques et les Russes ou les Allemands, entre la Pologne et la France etc.

Roland" et "Le Dit consacré à l'expédition des troupes d'Igor"), ou lorsqu'il parle de certains parallèles dans le domaine de la culture, de ceux résultant des influences aussi bien que de ceux ayant une source commune lointaine (p.ex. la fable).

Mickiewicz étudie les différences entre l'Occident et le Nord (les Slaves) sur l'exemple des trois composants de la civilisation qu'il tient pour les plus importants: la r e l i g i o n, la p o l i t i q u e, la c i v i l i s a t i o n. Il compare p.ex. des opinions de Rej et celles de Montaigne pour souligner les différences nées de la spécifité de "la même civilisation chrétienne, greffée d'un côté sur la Gaule romaine et de l'autre côté sur la société slave". (1.VI. 1841). Pourtant ni la proximité du "modèle idéal" (comme le croyaient les gens du Siècle des Lumières), ni l'originalité des phénomènes culturels (comme nous sommes portés à le faire) ne sont pour lui un critère. Le seul en est l'axiologie du christianisme. Il préfère donc l'"Histoire" de Długosz selon lequel "toute force réside en vérité" au système de Macchiavel, lorsqu'il compare ces historiens en prenant pour critère l'idée morale chrétienne. On voit le même critère dans la comparaison des différentes façons d'exercer le pouvoir royal et de l'obtenir. A propos de la libre élection, Mickiewicz écrit: "D'après la tradition chrétienne, d'après l'idée polonaise, idée connue de tous les peuples du Moyen Age, une élection était une opération tout autre que celle que l'on conçoit maintenant et qui a été formulée par Bentham, Rousseau et tous les publicistes modernes. Une élection, d'après l'idée de l'Eglise et de la nation polonaise, était un acte religieux; elle était considérée comme le résultat d'une influence immédiate de la Divinité, en un mot, comme un miracle". (8. XII. 1841).

A cette époque-là, l'Europe tendait vers des gouvernements fondés sur la r a i s o n (l'absolutisme), dit Mickiewicz, et elle savait créer un systeme stable d'une façon efficace. Il ne cache pourtant pas l'espoir qu'il sera possible, dans l'avenir, de créer un système fondé sur l'enthousiasme, sur les valeurs spirituelles et non sur les principes de la raison. Bien entendu, Mickiewicz se rend compte des faiblesses d'une telle civilisation (fondée sur l'esprit — "duch" —, sur l'enthousiasme et même sur la foi); le déclin de la Pologne le prouve. Mais, puisqu'il est Polonais, catholique et romantique, il y voit certaines valeurs ou bien certaines possibilités jusqu'ici non réalisées et qui font défaut à la "civilisation de la raison", c'est-a-dire à l'Occident. C'est à cause de la philosophie matérialiste qui s'appuie sur le principe rationnel, en dépit des valeurs chrétiennes, que l'Occident admire la tyrannie des tsars et justifie les actes de contrainte historique (Voltaire et Gibbon et les partages de la Pologne). A l'égard d'une telle attitude Mickiewicz n'éprouve que du mépris.

Le charme que "l'Orient mongol" avait pour l'Occident du XVIII-^{ème} siècle est une des peu nombreuses manifestations du r a p p o r t c o n s c i e n t de l'Occident envers les Slaves. L'Europe les ignore par principe et elle les attire, malgré leur complexe d'inferiorité et en dépit de la peur du ridicule. Cependant l'Occident pourrait apprendre beaucoup de choses des Slaves, s'il voulait bien regarder leur "vie pratique" avec une égale attention que celle que les Slaves consacrent aux théories de l'Occident. Ce dernier aurait pu, peu-être, s'épargner certaines tentatives d'appliquer ses théories, s'il avait su auparavent ce qui allait en résulter.

Ces Slaves que l'Europe dédaigne et qu'elle ne veut pas admettre dans la communauté ont cependant, d'après Mickiewicz, un rôle important à jouer. Ils l'espèrent (Kollar) de même que l'Europe l'espère, elle aussi (Herder). Car le XIX-ème siècle tout entier recherche une grande idée commune. La slavophilie naissante constituait précisément une telle recherche, dit Mickiewicz; il précise aussi quelles sont les valeurs qui devraient lui donner jour. Il en parle en citant un incident significatif où le père Marc, chef de la confédération de Bar, homme saint, a été sauvé par les soldats russes, habitués à obéir aux ordres et connus pour leur cruauté. "Les peuples slaves doivent y refléchir; ils pourraient y voir la preuve qu'il n'y a qu'une seule idée et qu'un seul principe qui puisse leur inspirer une sympathie commune: une idée religieuse, un principe religieux". (18. II. 1842).

Et pourtant le désir de l'idée commune n'est pas un symptôme de cosmopolitisme. C'est justement le dégoût de la littérature cosmopolite du siècle précédent qui implique la tendance à créer, au XIX-ème siècle, une littérature slave générale. Car c'est seulement la littérature nationale (et cela veut dire parfois — slave) qui peut être véhicule de cette grande idée que l'Occident pourrait accepter. Et quand une telle idée aura vu le jour, les différences entre l'Europe qui s'isole d'eux et les Slaves qui y aspirent disparaîtront. Il y aura lieu de retourner aux sources communes de la civilisation: aux valeurs chrétiennes. Mickiewicz, même lorsqu'il a recours à des visions prophétiques du retour futur de l'unité mythique, n'abandonne pas sa conviction que la particularité culturelle est une valeur: seule la nation qui y parviendra, aura quelque chose à offrir aux autres.

La Pologne

Quand Mickiewicz parle des Slaves à l'Occident il ne peut pas passer sous silence sa propre nation. Il est donc question des relations de la Pologne avec d'autres Slaves (particularité au sein de l'unité) et avec l'Europe Occidentale. On y verra aussi les tentatives de déterminer sa propre identité nationale. Regardons ce que Mickiewicz estime comme décisif pour la définition de la nation; c'est en même temps le trait qui détermine la communauté de race. C'est la forme du gouvernement et le système politique; la façon dont coexistent (socialement et politiquement) les individus. Le système qui résulte de la tradition propre à la nation est sa meilleure caractéristique, son trait distinctif. Le poète juge dangereux de s'approprier les idées politiques d'une autre nation, car cela peut conduire à la chute. Il cite, à tître d'exemple, la catastrophe nationale qu'a été l'acceptation par l'Etat polonais du Ier partage de la Pologne (ctd. le fait d'avoir reconnu comme acte légal la perte des territoirs appartenant à la Pologne). Puisque, dit-il, "(...) la Pologne n'avait fait aucune conquête, s'était formée par la réunion volontaire de plusieurs provinces au corps de la République (...) La Pologne, en abandonnant une seule de ses provinces, reniait la loi sur laquelle était fondée son existence". (8. III. 1842).

Mickiewicz présente d'une façon intéressante la façon dont le sens national et la notion de la patrie se sont éveillés chez les Polonais. Ce qui semble y avoir contribué, c'est la menace constante de la part des Turcs (au XVIII-ème siècle). Elle a permis à la nation de se consolider autor du sentiment de patriotisme accompagné du "sentiment de la puissance nationale" et de "l'idée de la vocation européenne de leur Etat". Cette vocation, c'était "la défense du christianisme et de la civilisation contre l'islamisme (sic!) et la barbarie". Ainsi donc le sens de l'identité nationale des Polonais accompagne, dès le début, la conviction qu'ils appartiennent à l'Europe et qu'ils ont la mission de défendre les valeurs fondamentales de celle-ci. Mickiewicz insiste sur le caractère immatériel de la notion de patrie chez les Polonais; l'accent mis sur la patrie en tant qu' "Etat de la race élue" (chez Skarga), "l'ordre social futur" (chez certains réformateurs contemporains au poéte) ou bien "l'idée de communauté privée d'Etat", semblable à l'Eglise catholique qui reconnaît des diocèses même formellement inexistants.

Le sens national des Polonais ne s'est pas uniquement formé à travers le contact (=le conflit) avec l'Orient, mais aussi, bien sûr, à travers le contact avec l'Europe Occidentale. Mickiewicz, lorsqu'il décrit l'influence de Rome et de Paris sur la Pologne et le déclin de l'Europe au XVII-ème, dit: "Comme partie de l'Europe, la république de Pologne partageait le sort des Etats avec lesquels elle était liée par sa politique et dont elle a été aussi la force morale et intellectuelle". (29. VI. 1841). D'ailleurs, le fait d'être une partie de l'Europe a eu parfois des conséquences négatives. Lorsque, par exemple, la Pologne a voulu mettre en pratique le principe — non formulé — de la non-intervention (Constitution du 3 mai 1791), elle a vu que l'Europe (= la Prusse et l'Autriche alliées à la Russie) ne le permettrait pas (le Ier partage de la Pologne). A ce propos et à propos d'autres choses aussi, Mickiewicz souligne les liens particuliers entre la Pologne et la France; historiques, réels (le Ier partage et la Révolution) aussi bien que "spirituels", consistant à partager l'idée de la révolte, de la révolution, de la liberté, le refus de la tyrannie: "la cause de ces nations est indissolublement liée dans les idées populaires" (12. IV. 1842). Il faut y ajouter que la question des relations entre la France et la Pologne, les Slaves, va dominer le 4e cycle des cours de Mickiewicz (1843-44), pour prendre une tournure mystique et prophétique que je laisse de côté. Certaines idées libérales et révolutionnaires, communes à la France et à la Pologne, trouvent un ennemi naturel en Russie. Il faut préciser tout de suite que Mickiewicz consacre relativement peu de place aux Slaves du Midi, qu'il parle avec estime des Tchèques, mais qu'il considère comme terminé leur rôle dans l'histoire de l'Europe contemporaine. Les Slaves sont pour lui surtout deux nations diamétralement opposées, rivales et en lutte l'une contre l'autre: les Russes et les Polonais. La Pologne a toujours incarné l'idée opposée à celle de la Russie, dit Mickiewicz, et il en donne plusieurs exemples. Il choisit deux périodes simultanées en Pologne et en Russie et il montre la terreur d'Ivan le Terrible et le libéralisme de Sigismond August, pour comparer la tyrannie en Russie et la liberté et la tolérance en Pologne. A cause des contrastes entre la Pologne et la Russie, à cause de toute la tradition de leurs hostilités historiques, il perçoit ces deux nations comme deux chevaliers du Moyen Age qui mènent un combat acharné pour défendre leurs idéaux aux yeux de l'Europe. La victoire de l'un des deux décidera de la forme future de l'Europe. Mickiewicz la met en garde contre un "flirt" avec le despotisme russe; il avertit que, en fait, il existe un gouffre entre l'Europe et la Russie. Ce gouffre résulte du fait que la Russie n'accepte pas le principe du légitimisme, du respect de la loi, et qu'elle ne le pratique pas, même si, paradoxalement, elle fait semblant de le défendre.[5]

Comme nous le voyons, la recherche d'une grande idée dans le Nord impose à l'Europe le choix entre deux tendances, représentées par deux grandes nations slaves. Mickiewicz cherche l'argument pour la thèse que c'est de la Pologne et non de la Russie que viendra cette idée, dans le domaine de l'axiologie religieuse et politique. "(...) un instinct religieux pur et profond (qui) ne se contentera, certes, d'aucune des formes politiques connues jusqu'à présent" (17. V. 1842), "un caractère chevaleresque et aventurier" — voilà des traits de la nation polonaise qui la prédestinent à jouer un grand rôle dans la formation d'une nouvelle "forme de gouvernement politique", plus parfaite. La condition de la littérature contemporaine, qui correspond au "ton" actuel de la nation, est un argument supplémentaire. Le caractère décadent de la littérature

---

5 P. ex. lorsqu'elle s'est prononcée contre la Grande Révolution Française, pour la monarchie.

russe, dit-il, ne promet pas de nouvelle idée; Pouchkine termine une époque. Par contre, en Pologne, après 1830, on a commencé à créer des oeuvres originales et la philosophie, en formulant les idées politiques en théories, leur donne un caractère général. Tout cela laisse espérer que ce sera la littérature polonaise qui donnera à l'Europe cette grande idée attendue. On pourra l'admettre comme généralement slave, étant donné que c'est l'esprit ("duch") et non la raison qui en est la valeur fondamentale. De plus, Mickiewicz annonce que cette idée est déja née: c'est le m e s s i a n i s m e ("ton polonais") qui peut aider à régénérer tous les Slaves aussi bien que l'Occident, si ce dernier l'accepte et l'adopte: "Ainsi, toute la marche politique et philosophique de l'Europe se trouve diamètralement opposée à la marche politique et religieuse de la Pologne". (29. VI. 1841). La preuve? La glorification de la Raison (par Hegel), divinité suprême de l'histoire, divinité despotique à la manière du despotisme russe. Mickiewicz ne perd tout de même pas l'espoir que l'Occident choisira la "solution polonaise" qui résulte de ce qu'il y a de plus précieux en Europe. Et c'est le christianisme qui est traitée comme la plus chrétienne des nations européennes — c'est donc à elle de donner l'idée que la nation la plus orthodoxe des nations slaves (qui "appliquait l'esprit chrétien et la forme catholique à la conduite politique", 14. VI. 1842) mettra en pratique. La Russie qui, comme l'Espagne, s'est toujours soucié du vrai rite (prawoslawna) plutôt que de l'esprit chrétien, développera dans le futur "la forme palpable, extérieure de cette vérité". Et de cette façon le rôle que les Slaves doivent jouer les rapprochera de l'Europe à laquelle ils appartiennent. Ce rôle permettra à l'Occident et au Nord de sauver en commun ce qu'ils ont de plus précieux ainsi que de créer du nouveau dans la politique aussï bien que dans la culture. Car, dit Mickiewicz, "Les temps sont passés où les nations disaient: Chacun chez soi, chacun pour soi. En quoi consisterait le progrès des nations si elles ne tendaient pas vers la construction d'une unité religieuse, politique et sociale?" (27. VI. 1843).

Conclusion

Ces idées de Mickiewicz au sujet de la domination des nations, de leur mission historique, du messianisme, le situent nettement au XIX-ème siècle et elles nous laissent plutôt sceptiques. Il ne faut tout de même pas oublier qu'elles partent des principes (des prémisses) qui méritent certainement une réflexion de l'homme contemporain. Il serait sans doute intéressant de réfléchir sur ce que Mickiewicz considère comme d é t e r m i n a n t s de l'i d e n t i t é n a t i o- n a l e. La r e l i g i o n, traitée comme la source de l'axiologie acceptée par la nation, en est le premier. Le second déterminant de la nationalité, le système politique de l'Etat, est strictement lié à la religion et dépend directement de ses normes morales. La littérature enfin, la plus importante branche de la culture spirituelle (d'après Mickiewicz) est le troisième déterminant. Il est significatif que Mickiewicz-romantique, chantre de l'extrême individualisme romantique, présente dans ses cours la littérature non pas tellement en tant qu'oeuvre de l'"esprit", de l'"inspiration" individuelle, mais plutôt comme le produit de la situation historique, un reflet de la religion et du système politique dominant dans cette nation que la littérature — selon le principe du cercle bouclé- devrait former. Car la littérature est responsable de la nation, de son aspect spirituel et réel. Ni le language commun, ni l'Etat, ni même le territoire commun habité ne sont indispensables à l'existence de la nation, pense Mickiewicz. Ce qui conditionne la particularité nationale, le caractère national, la stabilité de l'Etat et la permanence de la culture, c'est la continuation de sa propre tradition. Mickiewicz s'oppose à la transplantation des modèles étrangers qui ne résultent pas directement de la tradition propre à une nation, car cela fait perdre son identité et commettre de graves erreurs dans la politique ainsi que dans l'art. Cela ne veut pas dire qu'il faut s'isoler — il est juste et raisonable de prendre en considération les expériences des autres — dans tous les domaines. Lorsqu'il parle de la particularité nationale, Mickiewicz emploie une notion marquée par le temps et par le lieu — celle du ton (caractere national?). Ce n'est pas, malgré les apparences, une notion si irrationnelle qu'elle paraisse, car le "ton" est un produit du développement historiquee de la nation et non de facteurs nonhistoriques. Une autre notion, celle de la mission nationale (du rôle à jouer dans l'histoire) y est liée. Elle y est conçue (malgré une rhetorique ou une forme agaçantes) dans l'esprit herderien.

Mickiewicz essaie de définir en quoi consiste l'unité de l'Europe; ses essais paraissent très actuels aujourd'hui. Il énumère plusieurs déterminants de la communauté européenne. L'Europe Occidentale et les Slaves sont naturellement unis par des principes religieux et moraux communs qui sont le germe des liens futurs, peut-être plus étroits encore. Malgré les différences qui séparent des nations, il y a des éléments de la tradition commune qu'on peut et qu'il faut développer.Et c'est justement la fameuse idée commune de l'Occident et du Nord qui peut -et doit- être le lien le plus important dans l'avenir; idée déduite de leurs principes religieux et moraux qui transformera la vie des nations européennes dans l'esprit des valeurs chrétiennes.

Mickiewicz apprécie tout particulierement la liberté et la fidélité, des valeurs héritées du christianisme, qu'il tient pour les plus importantes. Il les croît opposées à la violence et à l'imitation irréfléchie des solutions des autres. Ce sont justement les principes de liberté et de fidelité, réalisés au cours des siècles dans des formes de gouvernements de la nation polonaise, qui constituent ces valeurs précieuses auxquelles il faut se référer lorsqu'on essaie de trouver des solutions historiques nouvelles et plus parfaites. Vu le manque de liberté extérieure, les Polonais devraient, dit Mickiewicz, mettre plus d'accent sur la liberté intérieure et sur la f i d e l i t é à l e u r p r o p r e t r a d i t i o n h i s t o r i q u e. La nation polonaise pourra jouer alors son rôle dans l'histoire de la Slavie et de l'Europe sans perdre le "ton" qui lui est propre.

Le souci de garder s a p r o p r e i d e n t i t é n a t i o n a l e va de pair avec la tendance à créer (maintenir) la c o m m u n a u t é. Mickiewicz en donne l'exemple lorsqu'il souligne la "coopération" de la France, de la Pologne et même de la Russie quant à la création-formation-ritualisation de l'"idée commune". L'accentuation du rôle de la Pologne ne devraient pas être traitée comme un simple essai de chanter les louanges de sa propre nation. Mickiewicz est persuadé que la Pologne a quelque chose à offrir à l'Europe; grâce à son héritage historique (par moments elle à réussi a se faire un système politique proche des i d é a u x c h r é t i e n s d e l' é p o q u e) ainsi que grâce à son héritage spirituel (qui se révèle surtout dans des oeuvres littéraires et philosophiques de ses contemporains, oeuvres issues des mêmes idéaux). La Pologne, croit-il, a une chance de suivre et continuer ce que l'Europe chrétienne a produit de plus noble au cours des siècles et, en y ajoutant sa propre empreinte, de proposer des solutions nouvelles, importantes non seulement pour elle.

Abstraction faite de tout ce qui semble être une compensation évidente des souffrances de la nation handicapée, on peut trouver dans les réflexions de Mickiewicz (si l'on ne prend pas ses opinons au pied de la lettre) une certaine actualité. Un contraste (une tension), une opposition entre l'Europe Occidentale et l'Europe Orientale (Centrale? — slave dans sa plus grande partie) ont persisté. Cette autre Europe ne cesse pas d'être pour l'Occident un défi, un point de repère par rapport auquel il faut se définir, une source d'inquiétude morale parfois. C'est pour cela qu'il vaut la peine de consacrer une attention soutenue à des conceptions de la culture et de l'histoire, du nationalisme et de l'européanisme nées dans l'esprit d'un poète d'il y a 150 ans, mais qui concernent une situation qui n'a pas tellement changé depuis.

Anna Drzewicka — Université Jagellonne, Cracovie

La "Chanson de Roland" en polonais: adoptions et refus d'un idéal

Quoi qu'on affirme sur l'altérité de la civilisation médiévale par rapport à la mentalité moderne, il ne semble pas que la *Chanson de Roland*, depuis sa redécouverte à l'époque romantique, se soit jamais laissé confiner au rôle du vénérable monument littéraire d'un temps révolu. Vivante et proche dans son éloignement même, elle n'a pas cessé de fasciner et de passionner. Oserai-je dire qu'elle était faite tout particulièrement pour passionner les Polonais? Assez récemment, A.W. Labuda a montré dans une étude intéressante[1] combien le topos de la mort héroïque, dont le *Roland* offre un modèle exemplaire, se retrouve sous forme de variantes diverses dans la littérature polonaise (Sienkiewicz, Żeromski, Andrzejewski), sans qu'il soit, évidemment, question d'influence; c'est là constater une affinité qui n'est sans doute pas fortuite.

La *Chanson de Roland* a eu en Pologne trois traductions intégrales, sans compter les fragmentaires, et de nombreuses rééditions. Traducteurs et éditeurs ont souvent muni leur texte de préfaces où, tout en offfrant à leurs lecteurs un certain nombre de renseignements historiques ou philologiques selon l'état de recherches de leurs époques respectives en même temps soit la motivation de leur choix, soit leur finalité, ou de faire passer un jugement de valeur non exclusivement esthétique et émis d'une perspective qui était la leur: polonaise. La *Chanson de Roland* en polonais: pourquoi? pour qui? accompagnée de quelles réactions de celui qui mettait sa peine pour rendre le chef-d'oeuvre de la France médiévale accessible à ses compatriotes du XIXe ou du XXe siècle? C'est à travers ces énoncés auto-commentateurs, mais aussi, partiellement — tâche plus délicate! — à travers la manière même de traduire que nous allons chercher une réponse à ces questions.

L'édition princeps du meilleur texte de la *Chanson de Roland* retrouvé à Oxford par Francisque Michel date, on le sait, de 1837. Moins de trente ans après, en 1866, une traduction polonaise paraissait, signalée dès 1880 par Léon

---

1 Cf. A. W. Labuda, *Apoteoza Rolanda i polska topika bohaterskiej śmierci*, Pamiętnik Literacki, 78, 1987/2, p. 61-89.

Gautier comme la quatrième traduction étrangère en date, précédée seulement de deux versions allemandes et d'une anglaise.[2] Son auteur était une femme, Seweryna Duchińska, récemment réfugiée à Paris après l'insurrection de 1863. Ecrivain médiocre mais travailleuse infatigable de la plume, elle allait accomplir une tâche considérable de vulgarisation des littératures occidentales en Pologne, entre autres à travers la revue de Varsovie, *Biblioteka Warszawska*, où fut publiée aussi sa traduction du *Roland*.[3] Dans l'introduction qui la précède on retrouve l'écho des théories ethno-historiques de l'époux de la traductrice, Franciszek Duchiński, et du baron Adolphe d'Avril, auteur de la version modernisée du texte dont elle s'était servie pour traduire. Ces théories insistaient sur l'unité ethnique et culturelle des peuples "arya-européens", depuis l'Inde jusqu'en Europe — y compris, pour Duchiński, les Slaves occidentaux: reléguant par contre la Russie moscovite à l'héritage d'une civilisation de nomades mongoles, il prenait une attitude nettement anti-panslaviste.

Or, c'est dans la même ligne que la traductrice, développant les idées de d'Avril — duméziliennes avant la lettre? — sur la communauté d'esprit et de conception de l'épopée aryenne — hindoue, persane, grecque, germanique, jusqu'à la *Chanson de Roland* qui n'en serait pour rattacher à la même grande famille les héros des légendes polonaises: Piast, Krakus ou Wanda. Elle formulait le souhait de contribuer par traduction à ranimer les recherches négligées sur tels personnages. Elle allait jusqu'à affirmer la supériorité de Krakus sur Roland: le premier des deux "touche moins à la réalité terrestre" et s'élève au status mythique du "héros rayonnant" combattant le mal personnifié par le dragon, tel Ormuzd contre Ahriman, tel Râma contre Râvana aux dix têtes ... Ainsi, faisant connaître aux lecteurs polonais une chanson de geste française de la fin du XIe siècle, Duchińska élargissait infiniment son horizon spatio-temporel, mais en même temps servait une cause très nationale: il s'agissait bel et bien de découvrir nos racines, d'affirmer l'identité européenne, occidentale de notre tradition cuturelle.

La même tendance apparaît d'ailleurs également là où, sans aborder le vaste terrain de l'étude comparée des civilisations, la traductrice-préfacière se concentre

---

2 Cf. L. G a u t i e r, *Les Epopées françaises*, t. III, 2e éd., Paris, 1880, p. 515, 533; idem, *Bibliographie des chansons de geste*, Paris, 1897, p. 176.

3 *Pieśń o Rolandzie*, in: Biblioteka Warszawska 1866, t. I, p. 1-49, 184-242. (introduction p. 1-33). L'épisode de Baligant, qui y manque, fut également traduit par Duchińska et publié la mčme année dans la revue "Kłosy" (1866, t. III, nos 66-69) sous le titre: *Bitwa pod Saragossą* (*La Bataille de Saragosse*). — L'auteur de la présente communication a jadis publié une étude sur la traduction de Duchińska: A. D r z e w i c k a, *Pierwszy polski przekład "Pieśni o Rolandzie"*, Zeszyty Naukowe Uniwersytetu Jagiellońskiego 112, 1965, p. 141-191, complété par: *Jak powstał najstarszy polski przekład "Pieśni o Rolandzie"*, Kwartalnik Neofilologiczny 12, 1965, p. 145-156.

davantage sur l'oeuvre traduite elle-même. Tout en relevant ses valeurs d'art et en la déclarant "digne d'être connue dans notre littérature" et apte à "relever dans notre pays les idées sur les vraies conditions de la beauté poétique" — tout en explicitant, donc, son intention pédagogique sur le plan proprement littéraire, elle insistait en même temps sur la "proximité" entre le lecteur polonais et ce poème, oeuvre "du peuple qui nous est le plus proche parmi tous les Aryens par une parenté spirituelle". Cette fois-ci, il s'agit d'affinités moins légendaires ou mythiques qu'historiques: la lutte contre les musulmans, trame importante dans l'histoire de Pologne depuis le XIIIe jusqu'au XVIIe siècle; Roland et Olivier en tant que correspondants de nos Sieciech ou Zawisza, et leurs adversaires en tant que "ceux que nous connaissons: des Osman, des Bajazet, des Soliman", etc. Il serait exagéré de dire que la *Chanson de Roland* devenait ainsi une épopée nationale polonaise, mais on s'y retrouvait en pays de connaissance.

Il en résulte que l'engagement guerrier des héros de la Chanson, leur lutte et leur sacrifice, étaient censés éveiller un écho dans les coeurs des destinataires appartenant à un peuple au lendemain de la débâcle mais toujours riche du souvenir héroïque de son passé, germe d'avenir. Traduction "pour conforter les coeurs'? On est en tout cas frappé de remarquer combien cette version en vers, non dépourve d'élan poétique mais assez étrangère aux rigueurs de la translation modernes et côtoyant parfois la paraphrase, prend ça et là, au niveau de l'expression, une coloration polonaise. Lorsque les héros francs pour insulter leur ennemi le traitent de "chien de païen" ("pies pogański") ou lorsque les Sarrasins invoquent le nom d'Allah complètement ignoré des chansons de geste ("Allah! — pogaństwo hurmem zawrzasło"), on plonge dans un univers analogue mais différent, déplacé nettement vers l'Est. De même quand, pour: "Frappez-les, chevaliers" on entend: "Rąbcie, Frankowie! kto w Boga wierzy!" (sur le modèle de l'idiome polonais traditionnel: "frappe qui croit en Dieu"), ou quand les païens crient: "Hejże na Franki" ("sus aux Francs"), exactement comme les petits nobles de *Messire Thadée* de Mickiewicz criaient, au cours d'un différend entre voisins, "Hajże na Soplicę!". L'assimilation, qu'elle soit recherchée ou inconsciente, devient comme un signe de l'identification spirituelle entre le poéme français et ses lecteurs polonais à travers la traduction de Duchińska.

Remarquons en passant qu'une démarche analogue de quasi-appropriation polonisante fut entreprise par Stefan Żeromski lui-même qui fit à la traduction de Duchińska l'honneur d'en citer quelques brefs fragments dans ses *Cendres*[4], en établissant un lien secret entre l'épopée lointaine de Roncevaux

---

4 Cf. S. Żeromski, *Popioły*, t. III, Warszawa, 1948, p. 22-23 (in: Pisma, pod redakcją S. Pigonia, t. IX).

et celle, vécue par son héros Krzysztof Cedro, de l'expédition napoléonienne en Espagne. Parcourant avec son régiment les routes "de la douce France" versles Pyrénées, le jeune homme se rend compte qu'il suit le chemin même de Charlemagne et devient obsédé par le souvenir de la Chanson de Roland (dont le texte d'Oxford restait encore inconnu à l'péoque de Napoléon, ce qui n'a, d'ailleurs, aucune importance), souvenir de "cette chanson qui a échappé lorsque les peuples avec leur histoire ont disparu' ("pieśni owej, co uszła cało" — citation cachée de Mickiewicz!). Rêve poétique d'héroïsme, désir d'accomplir des "actes de Roland et de Turpin", et même identification implicate des deux empereurs, celui à la barbe blanche d'il y a dix siecles et celui qui catalyse tout l'espoir actuel des Polonais. A la question posée jadis par le roi Marsile à propos de Charlemagne: "Quand sera-t-il las de guerroyer?", le jeune lancier de Napoléon répond spontanément, en adoptant le même rythme des décasyllabes: "Jamais, avant que la foi du peuple ne s'accomplisse et me fasse son oeuvre" ("Aż się ludowa wypełni wiara i spełni swoje..."). Espoir enthousiaste que la réalité de la guerre d'Espagne va démentir cruellement. Penché sur le cadavre nu d'un ami mort sans honneur, Krzysztof prononcera les paroles amères: "Voilà notre Roncevaux, compagnon".[5] Le poème de l'héroïsme glorieux de la vieille France devient un miroir déformant où se reflète le tragique du destin de la Pologne.

L'usage qu'en a fait Żeromski, ainsi que d'autres témoignages, prouvent que la version poétique de Duchińska a fait pendant longtemps fonction de la *Chanson de Roland* polonaise.Une autre traduction, en prose, d'après l'adaptation moderne de Léon Clédat, a été donnée en 1903 par Kazimierz Król[6], pédagogue et vulgarisateur très actif. Si l'introduction qui la précède se limite à fournir au lecteur quelques renseignements historiques et littéraires, il n'en va pas de même dans la deuxième édition de ce texte parue en 1921.[7] Le traducteur y ajoute une préface plus personnelle, où des réflexions sur les raisons de la popularité du vieux poème médiéval en France l'amènent à expliciter ses propres intentions. Il insiste sur l'actualité jamais dépassée pour l'esprit humain de la valeur de l'héroïsme "se révélant soit par des actes de prouesse militaire, soit par d'autres sortes de courage", ou bien du motif de la "lutte des éléments de la lumière et du bien contre ceux du mal et des ténèbres". Ces valeurs universelles, "éternellement fraîches" pour les hommes de tous les temps et de

---

5 Ibid., p. 274. — Cf aussi M. S t r z a ł k o w s k a, *Żeromski o Hiszpanii*, in: Stefanowi Żeromskiemu w setną rocznicę urodzin (Zeszyty Naukowe Wyższej Szkoły Pedagogicznej w Katowicach, 34), Katowice, 1967, p. 199-201.

6 *Pieśń o Rolandzie*, poemat średniowieczny francuski, opracował według oryginału Kazimierz K r ó l, Warszawa, 1903.

7 Idem, wydanie drugie, Poznań-Warszawa, 1921 (préface de la deuxième édition p. 1-4).

tous les peuples, rejoignent dans la *Chanson de Roland* un reflet des traits positifs du caractère national des Français: "droiture des sentiments, fidélité inflexible aux devoirs envers Dieu, les autorités, la nation et les personnes, respect profond de l'honneur, prouesse gurrière enfin, unie à un dévouement total et sans réserve". Ce qui fait des personnages rolandies une incarnation de l'idéal français; ils sont des héros nationaux, et la *Chanson* elle-même — un poème national. Le traducteur avoue qu'en publiant sa version polonaise en 1903 il visait un but d'éducation et de vulgarisation ("il est utile, pour une formation universelle de son esprit national, de prendre aussi connaissance de l'esprit des autres nations"); mais il a cru opportune une réédition "maintenant, lorsque les qualités de l'esprit français viennent encore de se révéler sans faiblir par des actes admirables, important à toute l'humanité". Ainsi, au lendemain de la première guerre mondiale, un enthousiasme francophile trouvait à s'exercer de plus, le sentiment de la parenté profonde, de la communauté d'idéal se fait bien sentir, quoique sous un aspect différent.

Il serait pourtant illusoire de considérer une telle attitude d'adhésion admirative et d'adoption de l'idéal rolandien comme naturelle et inévitable. Une dizaine d'années après, en 1932. la collection de traductions déja abondante, "Biblioteka Boya", s'enrichissait d'un texte nouveau de la *Chanson de Roland*[8], texte qui allait désormis devenir classique en Pologne. Importante par son envergure, la tâche de faire connaître aux Polonais une partie considérable de la littérature française entreprise par Tadeusz Żeleński (Boy) demandait à être complétée par la traduction du chef-d'oeuvre de l'épopée médiévale, accessible déjà à l'époque dans la belle version moderne de Bédier. Sans être parfaite, la version polonaise en prose qu'en a donnée à son tour Boy-Żeleński présentait, vu le talent exceptionnel du traducteur et sa puissance de travail, d'éminentes qualités littéraires. On peut cependant se demander si Boy ne s'était pas mis à cet ouvrage un peu à contrecoeur, ou, en tout cas, avec quelque ambivalence de réactions, dont on saisit l'écho dans son introduction au texte. L'attitude critique se révèle déjà sur le plan esthétique — les beautés de la *Chanson de Roland* y sont relevées comme présentes m a l g r é les imperfections d'un texte, en somme, plutôt pauvre et primitif; mais elle se fait incisive surtout sur le plan éthique. Boy parle de l'"impression étrange" que produit la lecture de la Chanson de Roland "aujourd'hui, au sortir de la grande guerre, à l'époque d'un *pacifisme* instinctif ou conscient". Les tentatives modernes d'actualiser l'idéal

---

8 *Pieśń o Rolandzie.* Wedle rękopisu oxfordzkiego w opracowaniu Józefa Bédier, przełożył i wstępem opatrzył Tadeusz Ż e l e ń s k i (Boy), Warszawa (1932), (préface du traducteur p. 5-10).

héroïque et guerrier provoquent sa réaction moqueuse: citant, sans le nommer, Léon Gautier[9] pour qui ce récit d'une grande défaite de la France réparée par une victoire glorieuse devenait source d'espoir après la débâcle de 1870, Boy suppose que dans les circonstances nouvelles, une fois le rêve de la victoire française réalisé, ce sont à leur tour les Allemands qui s'incitent peut-être à la vengeance par la légende de Charlemagne, héros germanique... Son ironie mordante ("toutes les nations de l'Europe — dit-il -sont combatives et courageuses, et chrétiennes, et le jour de la mobilisation, elles ont toutes Dieu de leur côté...") conduit cependant vers la découverte d'une autre actualité: celle des "petits détails", naguère inaperçus, et qui, d'après lui, impressionnent le lecteur contemporain — telle la mention de la cité de Galne que "le comte Roland ?...? avait prise et détruite; de ce jour elle resta cent ans déserte". Et Boy de se demander:

> "Pauvre cité de Galne...De quoi était-elle coupable/ Tout comme Einstein a vu la théorie de la gravitation avec les yeux de la pomme de Newton en train de tomber, ainsi l'homme d'aujourd' — hui regarde les exploits du preux Roland avec les yeux... de la cité de Galne. Ce "bulletin", à lui seul, entrera dans son coeur plus profondément que la formule glorieuse, bien des fois répétée, sur le chevalier qui a coupé en deux un autre chevalier à travers le heaume, le crâne, la tête, les dents, le corps, jusqu'à la selle, «sans lui faire d'autre mal»".[10]

Révolte, dit Boy; révolte de la poésie contemporaine, restée froide devant tout cet héroïsme dont l'Europe vient d'être le théâtre et auprès duquel "pâlissent les exploits de Charlemagne", à un moment où "n'importe quel employé ou savant, arraché à sa table de travail, se trouvait obligé de devenir un Roland". Les "habitants laborieux de la cité de Galine" préfèrent, comme héros, un Amundsen.

Ce refus énergique de l'homme et du critique a-t-il laissé intacte l'oeuvre du traducteur? Boy avait une capacité extraordinaire de s'adapter; d'autre part, ses traductions diverses accusent souvent une tendance à intensifier

---

9 Cf. *La Chanson de Roland*, texte critique, traduction et commentaire (...) par Léon Gautier, 11e éd., Tours, 1881, p. LII.

10 Ed. cit., p. 10. L'expression *seinz altre descunfisun*, traduite d'abord par Bédier; "sans lui faire d'autre mal", n'apparaït dans le texte d'Oxford qu'une fois (v.1894); dans une édition ultérieure Bédier a corrigé son texte en: "sans lui faire de blessure sanglante". Autre interprétation possible: sans être obligé de frapper un second coup.

l'expressivité des textes, à introduire des termes plus imagés ou plus dynamiques que dans les originaux. On ne s'etonne donc pas de retrouver le même procédé dans sa *Chanson de Roland.* Un soupçon s'éveille pourtant: cette insistance sur l'aspect violent et sanglant du poème n'est-il pas ici, un peu, une démarche de polémique implicite? Les héros du texte polonais, qualifiés de "tęgie zuchy" ou "tęgie chwaty" (mettons: "des braves à trois poils") semblent d'un tempérament encore plus sanguin que leurs modèles français. Ceux-ci "frappent", ceux-là "kropią" ou "walą" (walą krzepko", "walą co wlezie" — mettons, très approximativement; "ils tapent dur"). Là où Bédier rend les injures qu'ils prononcent par le terme "truand", Boy s'en donne à coeur joie: "nicpoń", "ladaco", "łajdak", "ścierwo". Inutile de retraduire: la balance penche vers une jovialité "sarmate" teintée de brutalité qui trahit peut-être, quoique non nécessairement, une rancune.

Rancune et révolte qui peuvent se comprendre: on ne saurait nier que la *Chanson de Roland* est un poème terrible du sang et de la violence. Mais le message d'héroïsme, de fidélité, de sacrifice suprême, qu'elle transmet en même temps à travers les siècles ne se laisse pas ébranler. Les rééditions nombreuses de la traduction de Boy seront accompagnées parfois d'autres préfaces, où des accents discrets d'une actualisation positive vont réapparaître, malgré les expériences, depuis encore plus sanglantes, de l'historie. En 1959, la préface de Krystyna Kasprzyk évoque le son de l'olifant qui, "malgré les conditions si différentes de la vie, ne cesse d'éveiller des échos assoupis dans chaque coeur, parlant tout bas de l'héroïsme, du dévouement, de la gloire".[11] En 1968, celle de Zygmunt Czerny affirme que de nombreux lecteurs, dans bien des pays, recherchent dans les chansons de geste "des mots-d'ordre encore actuels, chers à leurs arrière-grands-pères: patrie, honneur, courage, amitié, dévouement. C'est la le trésor le plus secret, mais toujours vivant de ces poèmes".[12]

Pour finir, écoutons non plus un traducteur ni un préfacier, mais un poète. Zbigniew Herbert, ou, plus exactement, son "Monsieur Cogito", prononce le nom de Roland. Il l'associe à ceux de Gilgamesh et d'Hector: "tes ancêtres", dit-il. Ancêtres de celui dont il exige un engagement total et absolu, au prix de l'anéantissement de soi. Ce sont eux, "défenseurs du royaume sans fin et de la cité de cendres" qui apparaissent comme guides et phares, avant que ne soit prononcé l'ordre irrévocable: "Sois fidèle va" —

---

[11] *Pieśń o Rolandzie*, przełożył Tadeusz Żeleński (Boy), Warszawa, 1959, p.8.

[12] *Pieśń o Rolandzie*, przełożył Tadeusz Żeleński (Boy), in: Arcydzieła francuskiego średniowiecza, Warszawa, 1968, p. 43.

Idź dokąd poszli tamci (...)
Idź bo tylko tak będziesz przyjęty do grona zimnych czaszek
Do grona twoich przodków: Gilgamesza Hektora Rolanda
Obrońców królestwa bez kresu i miasta popiołów

Bądź wierny idź[13]

---

[13] Z. H e r b e r t, Przesłanie pana Cogito.

Gabriela Matuszek — Jagiellonische Universität, Krakau

Die Rolle des Slawentums bei der Rezeption der Deutschen um die Jahrhundertwende XIX/XX

(Stanisław Przybyszewski als eine "echte slawische Erscheinung").

Stanisław Przybyszewski, ein Dichter, in dem die Deutschen einen Protagonisten der neuen Kunst erblickten und der in Polen den status dignitatis als Anführer der modernistischen Bewegung erhielt, gehört zweifellos zu dem Schöpferkreis, der den Dialog zwischen den Kulturen des Ostens und des Westens inspirierte. "Ein solcher aber, ein echter Sproß vom Stamme E. T. A. Hoffmanns, war Stanislaus Przybyszewsky, der polnisch-deutsche Dichter, der mystisch-ekstatische Slawe, der allerdiffirenzierteste Nervenmensch und tiefsinnigtolle Alkoholiker - und er eigentlich hat die letzte Berliner Bohème großen Stils geschaffen"[1] — erklärt Julius Bab in seinem Buch *Die Berliner Bohème*.

"Der geniale Pole", wie man Przybyszewski in Berlin nannte, war nicht nur spiritus rector des künstlerischen Lebens der Berliner, später auch Krakauer Bohème, der Katalysator der Umwandlungen in beiden Literaturen und Inspirator vieler schöpferischer Ideen — sondern spielte im literarischen Leben slawischer Länder (vor allem in Polen, Rußland und in Böhmen) die Rolle des "Fensters nach Europa", und den Deutschen erschloß er den "Weg zum Slawentum". Julius Meier-Graefe schreibt:

> "Stachu machte uns das Slawische auf — nicht das große Tor zu Dostojewski, vielmehr eine verborgene Tapetentür, von der man nicht wußte, ob sie ins Chaos oder in eine bewohnbare Landschaft oder nur in einen mit Mixturen gefüllten Wandschrank führte".[2]

In den Künstler-Kreisen Berlins der 90er-Jahre zeichnete sich die Gestalt des polnischen Dichters, der seine ersten aufregenden Dichtungen (*Totenmesse*,

---

1 J. Bab, *Die Berliner Bohème*, Berlin u. Leipzig 1905, S. 52.
2 J. Meier-Graefe, *Geschichte neben der Kunst*, Berlin 1933, S. 136-137.

Vigilien, Himmelfahrt, De profundis) in deutscher Sprache verfaßte, vor allem aus durch die Art seiner Schaffens, das erstarrte literarische Muster durchbrach, aber auch durch seine Exotik, die von den Deutschen vor allem mit der slawischen Natur des Autors *Zur Psychologie des Individuums* erklärt wurde. Für viele war er eine "echte slawische Erscheinung", und unter der Periphrasen, mit denen der für Deutsche schwer aussprechbare Name des polnischen Dichters umschrieben wurde, nehmen diejenigen einen beachtlichen Platz ein, in denen seine Zugehörigkeit zum Slawentum besonders unterstrichen wird wie "slawischer Strindberg" oder "Genie slawischer Rasse". Worin erblickte man also slawische Merkmale bei einem Künstler, der in gewissen Kreisen des Jungen Berlins als "König der Bohème", "Lockspitzel der Moderne" und "Dämon der jüngsten Literatur" funktionierte?

Die Andersartigkeit und Exotik des Ankömmlings aus dem Osten sah man bereits in seinem fremd klingenden Namen, von dem Bruno Wille mit großen Sinn für Humor folgendes schrieb: "sieben zischende Konsonanten mit dem Fistelgezwitscher des einen (!) Vokals — in echter Aussprache klang es fast wie "pschih!".[3] Die charakteristischen Gesichtszüge des blondes Kopfes des "polackischen Byrons" deuteten auf den slawischen Charakter seiner Physiognomie: "sein Gesicht, starke Backenknochen, zurückliegende Augen, flausiger Bart, kopf eines slawischen Christus, den man sich am Kreuz vvorstellen konnte, hatte zugleich Züge eines Berserkers".[4]

Die Vorstellung von den Slawen als barbarische Stämme, die vor allem von zur Expansion nach Osten drängende preusßschen Junkern verbreitet wurde, war zweifellos einer der Gründe für des Interesse, das diese exotische Erscheinung, der "wilde Pole voll von Dämonie" weckte. Das Verhalten des "genialen Polen" versetzte die an Ordnung gewöhnten Deutschen in Erstaunen, seine Exzesse, Auschreitungen, Straßenstreiche, Solo-Tänze in den Kneipen und leidenschaftliche Diskussionen zogen einen Kreis von faszinierten Anhängern an. Die nüchterne deutsche Natur fand in dieser Persönlichkeit voller Fermente und Unruhe eine interessante Alternative. Die slawische Offenheit und Direktheit in Kontakten mit anderen Menschen, die Fähigkeit, seine Gedanken auf interessante Art und Weise darzustellen, die seltene Gabe, sich in extatischen Improvisationen auszudrcüken und sich mit einer dämonischen Aura zu umgeben, lockten seine deutschen Freunde an. Eben er, dieser "wilde Slawe", "wurde nicht äußerlich das Haupt der Gelage im "Schwarzen Ferkel", er erfüllte auch innerlich die ganze Schar in geradezu dämonischer Weise mit

---

3 B. W i l l e, *Das Gefängnis zum Preusßschen Adler. Eine selbsterlebte Schildbürgerei*, Jena 1914, S. 136.

4 J. M e i e r - G r a e f e, *Geschichte neben der Kunst*, op. cit., S. 136.

seinem Geist — vielleicht der legitimste "König der Bohème", den Berlin seit Grabbes Tagen gesehen hat".[5]

Der den Slawen nachgesagte starke Alkoholkonsum bekam mit der Person Stanisław Przybyszewskis eine vollkommene Bestätigung. Heinrich Hart sah diesen Romantiker und Bohemien nie anders als im Rausch.[6] Das Epitheton "extremer Alkoholiker" disqualifizierte Przybyszewski allerdings nicht, da Alkohol das geistige Leben der Bohemien stimulierte, diente er ja auch der Befreiung von gesellschaftlichen Zwängen. Die slawische Inspiration spielte dabei eine unbestreitbar wichtige Rolle, besonders in den Kreisen der Friedrichshagener Bohème, wo sich nihilistische "russische" Anschauungen großer Popularität erfreuten. Davon zeugt zum Beispiel ein Pasguill, das sich auf die Anhänger dieser "russischen" Lebensweise bezog:

"Wir wollen uns mit Schnaps berauschen.
Wir wollen unsere Weiber tauschen,
Wir wollen uns mit Talg beschmieren
Im Sonnenscheine nackt spazieren —
Wir wollen echte Russen sein!"[7]

Der Unterschied zwischen dem "Homo ludens", den der "echte Slawe" für die Deutschen verkörperte und dem protestantischen "Homo faber" machte sich nicht nur in der Verhaltensweise bemerkbar.Einen tieferen Unterschied sah man in der Struktur der Persönlichkeit, die sonst die ganze Fülle von Reaktionen auf die äußeren Stimuli anregte.

Diese andersartige slawische Natur wurde als ein potentielles Korrektiv für den deutschen Charakter angesehen. Im Mentalitätsunterschied zwischen Slawen und Germanen sah man eher sich ergänzende Aspekte, als Widersprüche. Eine These von Dehmel über die *Totenmesse*, die eine "zeitpsychologische Ergänzung" zu Schlafs Frühling, "der negative Pol derselben Achse"[8] sei, wiederholt sich in den Urteilen vieler Kritiker. Nach Meinung Dehmels sind beide künstlerische Varianten: das affirmative Erleben der Wirklichkeit nach Johannes Schlaf und die Lebensverneigung des polnischen Autors, wie Saat und Dünger, aus denen eine neue Kunst geboren wird. Servaes verwies ebenfalls

---

5 J. B a b, *Die Berliner Bohème*, op. cit., S. 54.

6 H. H a r t, *Literarische Erinnerungen. Aufsätze*, in: *Gesammelte Werke*, Bd. 3, Berlin 1907, S. 91.

7 Zit. nach: St. P r z y b y s z e w s k i, *Moi współcześni. Wśród obcych*, Warszawa 1926, S. 71.

8 R. D e h m e l, *Brief an Bierbaum*, In: *Modernen Musenalmanach auf das Jahr 1894*, herausg. von O. J. Bierbaum, München 1894, S. 277.

darauf, daß die Neigung der beiden Dichter eigene Empfindungen mit den Naturkräften zu identifizieren, auf zwei verschiedene Weisen nach außen projiziert werden, die durch unterschiedliche geistige nationale Strukturen vorausgesetzt sind. Im Gegensatz zu Schlaf, der die Welt bis in die kleinsten Details hinein genießt, verliert sich Przybyszewski im makrokosmischen Raum.[9] Athur Moeller-Bruck stellt dem Schlafschen kosmologischen Optimismus den kosmologischen Pessimismus des polnischen Dichters gegenüber.[10] Spezifisch nationale Eigenheiten Przybyszewskis fassen auch die Kritiker ins Auge, die das Schaffen von Przybyszewski mit den Werken eines anderen Germanen, August Strindbergs, vergleichen. Der schwedische Dramatiker, von Natur aus Skeptiker, betrachtet mit Hohn sein Puppenspiel, das er überlegen lenke — bemerkt Ernst Schur.[11] Der Pole dagegen sei ein Gefühlsmensch, befindet sich immer in Gährung, gebe sich wie ein Vulkan. Seine Helden seinen kothurmässig und pathetisch wie in alten Sagen.

Die Persönlichkeit von Przybyszewski stimmte nicht nur mit srereotypen Vorstellungen von einem Slawen überein, sondern verkörperte auch ihre extreme Verbalisierung. Die slawische Empfindlichkeit und Sinnlichkeit, die Neigung zu extatischen Geisteszuständen, Überempfindlichkeit und Erregbarkeit waren — der Meinung deutscher Beobachter zufolge — für diesen polnischen "Rauschknüstler" charakteristisch. "Etwas Faszinierendes ging vom ihm aus, etwas Aufwühlendes, Suggestives" — schrieb 1896 Franz Servaes — "Lieber toll als nüchtern!" Er, er war toll in der siebenten Potenz, und nüchtren hat man ihn niemals gesehn".[12]

Explosion der Gefühle, riesengroße emotionelle Dimensionen, die in Przybyszewskis Werken zu finden sind, begeisterten die deutschen Leser. F. Oppeln-Bronikowski bemerkte, daß "diese Bücher reich an aparten Wendungen, überraschenden Bildern, kühnen Hyperbolen und leidenschaftlichen, heißen Gefühlen sind, wie alles, was der sensitive Pole schreibt".[13]

Dieses Schaffen war für Deutsche ein interessantes Konglomerat aus Extase und grenzenloser Melancholi, aus Sinnlichkeit und Pessimismus, Exaltierheit und Ironie. Die Verbindung von Gegensätzen, die nur im Rahmen der slawischen Natur möglich ist, fand in Przybyszewski einen besonders starken Ausdruck.

---

9 Vgl. F. S e r v a e s, *Vohinaus? Litterarische Rundschau*, In: "Neue Deutsche Rundschau (Freie Bühne)" 1894, S. 947.

10 Vgl. A. M o e l l e r - B r u c k, *Unser aller Heimat*, in: *Die moderne Literatur*. In Gruppen- und Einzelndarstellungen, Bd. 7, Berlin u. Liepzig 1900, s. 29-31.

11 E. S c h u r, *Neue Dramen von Przybyszewski*, In: Die Schaubühne 1908, Hf. 31/32, S. 81.

12 F. S e r v a e s, *Jung-Berlin. Zehn Jahre Literatur-Bewegung*, In: Die Zeit 1896, Hf. 114, S. 155.

13 F. O p p e l n - B r o n i k o w s k i, *Stanislaw Przybyszewski: "Epipsychidion"*. "In diesem Erdenthal der Tränen", In: Das literarische Echo 1899/1900, S. 1444-1445.

Diese slawischen Eigenschaften werden bei Przybyszewski quasi intensiviert, weil er — wie Alfred Neumann bemerkt[14] — Pole, also Vertreter der extremen Slawen ist. Diese Fähigkeit der Polen, verschiedene Gegensätze miteinander zu vereinbaren, stieß bei unseren westlichen Nachbaren kaum auf Bewunderung. Sie wurde eher als Anschein von Unproduktivität, geistiger Schwäche und Unfähigkeit gewertet, der polnischen Seele in ihrem Streben eine Richtung zu weisen und ihre intelektuellen und emotionellen Potenzen zu nutzen. Mit einem Wort, die für Deutsche bedeutsame Bezeichnung "Leistung" verliert in Beziehung auf den Polen ihren magischen Sinn.

Dieser Stereotyp vom "unproduktiven Polen", der im Bewußtsein der Deutschen funktionierte, schließt auch die Persönlichkeit Przybyszewskis mit ein.

> "Przybyszewski entsprach in vielem dem romanhaft ausgeprägten Typus des Polen — schreibt Julius Bab — der von extatischer Schwärmerei zu uferloser Melancholie taumelt, reich an allen möglichen sinnlichen und geistigen Gaben, aber ohne eigentlich sammelnder Kraft".[15]

Die Popularität seiner Werke ergab sich eben größtenteils aus der fehlenden organisierenden Kraft in der dargestellten Welt seiner Werke. Die Welt von Przybyszewski sei das Chaos, bemerkte E. Schur.[16] Die Explosion von Geisteszuständen im Unterbewußtsein zersprengt nämlich die Form der Werke und stellt traditionelle Gattungsnormen in Frage. Seine ersten Dichtungen waren für das deutsche Publikum eine echte überraschung: "das Buch selbst in seiner Art als ein Unikum in der gesamten modernen Literatur dasteht"[17] — schreibt Ola Hansson von der *Totenmesse.* Nach der Meinung von Kolokol: "das Buch steht einzig da in unserer Literatur, ich wüßte auch aus fremden Literaturen nichts mit ihm zu vergleichen".[18] Auch laut Franz Servaes: "In der That handelt es sich hier um eine literarische Erscheinung, die schlechtweg ohne Vorbild ist".[19]

Das Substrat des seltsamen schriftstellerischen Angesichts von Przybyszewski war — in den Aufassungen seiner deutschen Beobachter — das polnische Temperament, das Streben Przybyszewskis unaussprechbare Geistes-

---

[14] A. Neumann, *Der deutsche Roman und Stanislaus Przybyszewski* (*Ein Beitrag zur Geschichte des Snobismus*), In: Monatschrift für neue Literatur und Kunst, 1898, S. 462.

[15] J. Bab, *Richard Dehmel*, Leipzig 1926, S. 96.

[16] Vgl. E. Schur, *Neue Dramen von Przybyszewski*, op. cit., S. 81.

[17] O. Hansson, *Eine moderne Todtenmesse*, in: Die Nation 1893/94, S. 15.

[18] Kolokol, *Ein deutscher Sataniker*, in: Freie Bühne, 1893, Hf. XII, S. 1363.

[19] F. Servaes, *Wohinaus?*, op. cit., S. 947.

zustände, tiefen Schichten der Psychik vorzustellen, ins Unterbewußtseinverdrängten Inhalte aufzudecken, hatte seine Quelle ebenso in der polnischen Tradition der alternativen Gegenüberstellung der Vernunft und des Gefühls, der Glorifizierung irrationaler und spontaner Haltung.

Arthur Moeller-Bruck verbindet die spezifische Wesensart von Przybyszewskis Schaffen mit dem Katholizismus[20], obgleich in den Werken des Verfassers der *Synagoge des Satans* die Stelle des Katholizismus eine Religion à rebours, der Satanismus, einnimmt, der als eine spezifische Einstellung eines gegen Vorsehung und Leiden rewoltierenden Menschen wird. Auch wenn Przybyszewski das katholische Wertsystem negierte, der Pole und Katholik Stereotyp bei der Rezeption seiner Werke hervorgehoben wurde. Przybyszewskis Schaffen sah man als "die Vermischung vom katholischen Weihrauchdunst und Satanskult, von lyrischen Pathos und wissenschaftlicher Sezierungswut"[21] an. "Ein katholischer Dunst steigt auf, den protestantische Nerven nicht vertragen"[22], schreibt über seine Werke ein Rezensent der *Vigilien.* Zum Extrakt des Schaffens des polnischen Dichters erklärt Bierbaum in seinem spöttischen *Steckbriefen* "eines nach Jodoform riechender Katholizismus" und Schnäpsen, "auf denen die polnische Messe zelebriert wird".[23]

Der polnischen Literatur wird nicht nur die vom Katholizismus abgeleitete emotionale Sphäre, sondern auch die "künstlerische Weiche des Pathologischen"[24] zugeschrieben, was übrigens von den Deutschen als differentia specifica der slawischen Literatur empfunden wird. In den Grenzen des Pathologischen betrachtet man nämlich die in der Werken von Przybyszewski enthaltene Anerkennung des Leidens als Hauptdeterminante des menschlichen Daseins, die Verachtung der Wirklichkeit und Verneigung des Lebens, die Todesfaszination und die Neigung zur Selbstzerstörung.

Hinter der Destruktion und Vernichtung, die man in Przybyszewskis Werken vorfindet, verbirgt sich — den Interpreten zufolge — das ganze geschichtliche Fiasko der Polen.[25] Der Grund für diese Dekadenzstimmung, die die ersten Dichtungen des Autors der *Totenmesse* erfüllt, wird als "tragisch wirklich" bezeichnet. Seine Heimat ist nämlich das "triste, düstere, wühlende Polen".[26]

---

20 A. Moeller-Bruck, *Richard Dehmel*, in. Die moderne Literatur, op. cit. Bd. 6, Berlin u. Leipzig 1900, s. 42.

21 A. Soergel, *Dichtung und Dichter der Zeit. Neue Folge. Im Banne des Expressionismus*, Leipzig 1927, S. 16.

22 G. Morgenstern, *Stanisław Przybyszewski: Vigilien.* in: Die Gesellschaft 1895, S.116-117.

23 M. Möbius [O. J. Bierbaum], *Steckbriefe*, Leipzig 1900, S. 108.

24 Kolokol, *Ein deutscher Sataniker*, op. cit., S. 1363.

25 Vgl. F. Servaes, *Vohinaus?*, op. cit., S. 947.

26 A. Neumann, *Der deutsche Roman und Stanislaus Przybyszewski* op. cit., S. 460.

Denselben "polnischen Ton" nehmen die Kritiker in *Der tote Ton* von Kornel Ujejski wahr (von Dehmel mit Hilfe Przybyszewskis ins Deutsche übertragen), ihn erblickten sie im Bild von Wacław Szymanowski *Modlitwa* (*Das Gebet*), das in der Sezessionaustellung in München präsentiert wurde, oder erkennen sie in der Musik Chopin. Der Pessimismus Przybyszewskis erhält also eine genealogische Qualifizierung. In dieser Hinsicht ist die Beendigung des ausführlichen Aufsatzes von A. Moeller-Bruck über das Schaffen Przybyszewskis bezeichnend:

> "Was mußte das für ein Dichter gewesen sein, der in einer Zeit der weiten Weltfreude über seine Lippen nur Worte sandte, die qualvoller Sehnsucht, todtmüder Trauer oder irrsinniger Verzweiflung entsprangen?"[27]

Die Kosmische Glorifizierung des Leidens bei Przybyszewski, die zweifellos ihren Grund in der Philosophie von Schopenhauer hatte, ersetze das nationale Märtyrertum, was jedoch keineswegs bedeutet, daß Przybyszewski darauf verzichtete, die Deutschen mit polnischen Komplexen zu verblüffen. Przybyszewski teilte die Meinung, daß sich ein Pole in der europäischen Gemeinschaft fremd fühlt, betonte er doch seine Angehörigkeit zum Polentum auf eine besondere Weise. In seinen Werken erscheinen nämlich keine Gestalten aus dem nationalen Theater der Phantasien. Przybyszewski läßt sein Schaffen ganz bewußt außerhalb der Bilder und Symbole des polnischen Nationaluniversum. Für Przybyszewski lag das Polentum eher im Bereich der emotionellen und intelektuellen Potenz und die "polnische Seele", oder allgemeiner gasagt, die "slawische Seele", war nicht eine eigenartig chiffrierte Matrize, die lediglich für ein Mitgleid dieser Gemeinschaft lesbar war, sondern vor allem ein emotionell umrissenes Gebiet. Für ein im Nationalcharakter der Polen dominierendes Element hielt Przybyszewski "dieses heroisches Leiden, das mit einem vornehmen Lächeln verdeckt wird, das sich hinter tückischer Ironie und Narrengestik versteckt".[28]

Przybyszewski entwickelte auf wohl vollkommenste Weise die den Polen angeborene Neigung zur Wichtigtuerei, doch statt der Gestik des national-patriotischen Szenariums, erscheinen bei ihm Narrentum und Spott. Die todesmutigen Handlungen wurden durch Exzesse und Ausschreitungen, die Haltung eines Verschworenen durch den Status eines Zigeuners ersetzt. Sein

---

27 A. M o e l l e r - B r u c k, *Mysterien*, in: Die moderne Literatur, op. cit Bd. 5, Leipzig 1902, S. 47.

28 St. P r z y b y s z e w s k i, *Szlakiem duszy polskiej*, Poznań 1920.

Narrentum war jedoch eine Art Anzeichen von Anarchie, eine Reaktion auf erstarte Werte, darin fand der Aufruhr gegen die Normen, die das Individuum einschränken, statt. Dieses Narrentum des "verrückten Polen" wurde gerade am häufigsten von seinen deutschen Freunden kritisiert. In den belletristischen Schilderungen von Przybyszewski wird diese Eigenschaft besonders stark betont ("Der geniale Pole" wurde als ein Muster für viele literarische Helden in der deutschen Literatur genutzt[29]). Kasimir der Fugenorgler, eine der Romanfiguren aus Bierbaums *Stil*pe[30] wurde in der Gestik eines Narres dargestellt. Auf Przybyszewski spielte auch eine andere Gestalt von Bierbaum an — Goethinsky aus dem Roman *Prinz* Kuckuck. Goethinskys Maskerade wurde genutzt, um einige kritische Bemerkungen an Przybyszewskis Adresse zu richten:

> "Du hast keinen Sinn für tragische Sehnsucht. Du bist eine Figur aus dem Spielkasten der Kunst. Oder, um es anders zuwenden: Du bist ein moderner Knüstler. Das Leben ist dir zu groß, zu tief, zu heilig. Du machst ein Spiel darauf. Treibst allotria. Hast Trist nötig — d. h. Lüge, — d. h. Kunst".[31]

Andere nahmen unter der Narren-Maske Przybyszewskis versteckte Leidenschaften und Gefühle aber auch ein ausgeprägtes "Weltgefühl" wahr. "So gern und so geschickt auch Przybyszewski posiert, um Freunde über seine wahren Gemütsstimmungen zu täuschen..."[32], bemerkt Franz Sevaes. Julius Meier-Graefe in seiner Rezension über *Unterwegs* anerkannte die Narrheit als Konstruktionsdominante in seinen Werken.[33] Laut Laender: "Am schwierigsten ist es bei diesem Schriftsteller zu scheiden, wo die Ironie aufhört und der Ernst anfängt".[34]

Anstelle des romantischen Verschworenen und des positivistischen Mannes der Tat, finden wir bei Przybyszewski ein durch schmerzensreiches Lächeln verzerrtes Narrengesicht. Auch diese, vom Autor des *De profundis* in der Fin de siècle-Epoche vorgeschlagenen Variante des Polentums, kann als nächste Emanation des narzistischen Charakters der Polen empfunden werden. Przybyszewski war bestrebt, von den Deutschen für einen "interessanten Polen" gehalten zu werden; seine Narrengestik und die bis heute unerhörten Exzesse,

---

[29] Vgl. G. M a t u s z e k, *Wzorzec modnego pisarza. Stanisław Przybyszewski w utworach pisarzy niemieckich*, in: Pamiętnik Literacki 1989, Hf. 3.

[30] Vgl. O. J. B i e r b a u m, *Stilpe*, op. cit.

[31] O. J. B i e r b a u m, *Prinz Kukckuck. Leben, Taten, Meinungen und Höllenfahrt eines Wollustlings*, Berlin 1928, s. 453.

[32] F. S e r v a e s, *Wohinaus?*, op. cit., S. 947.

[33] Vgl. J. M e i e r - G r a e f e, *Stanisław Przybyszewski*, in: Die Gesellschaft 1895, S. 1044.

[34] L e a n d e r [K. Credner], *Kritik*, in: Die Gesellschaft 1896, S. 687.

mit denen er die an feste Ordnung gewöhnten Deutschen verblüffte, sollten einer Intensivierung des "Polenumreizes" dienen. Viele wurden tatsächlich davon angelockt. Przybyszewski vermochte es nämlich, eine unwiderholbare Aura um sich zu schaffen und von Natur aus kühlen Deutschen emotional in Wallung zu bringen.

Jener fast dämonische Einfluß Przybyszewskis auf seine Umgebung wurde vortrefflich in einem autobiographischen Roman seines damals engen Freunds, Franz Servaes *Gährungen*[35], sichtbar gemacht. Spiridion Krakuscheck, "Genie der slawischen Rasse", wurde als eine außergewöhnliche Erscheinung vorgestellt. Die Berliner Künstler erlagen dem Reiz seiner fesselnden Persönlichkeit. Seine Meinungen wurden als eine Offenbarung der neuen Wahrheit aufgenommen.

Dieser mystisch-ekstatische Slawe, wie Przybyszewski bezeichnet wurde, stimulierte zweifelsohne das geistige Leben der Berliner Bohème. Ein gewisser "Poloniesierungs-Prozess" des künstlerischen Milieus könnte sich vollzogen haben, wenn Servaes später eine neue Schaffensperiode Dehmels als "Entpolonisierung" begrifflich bestimmte.[36] Die Bezeichnung "chopinisieren", die zum Synonym für nichtkonventionelle Gesten und Verhaltensweisen, aber auch literarischer Sprachexperimente wurde, war sprichwörtlich unter der Berliner Bohème. Die Enthüllung der "polnischen Seele" wurde in bedeutenden Maße durch die Musik von Chopin realisiert.

Przybyszewski drängte schon in seinem ersten Aufsatz, der dem jungen Literaten einen gewissen Ruf einbrachte, den Deutschen eigene Interpretationsweise des Schaffens dieses hervorragenden polnischen Komponist auf. Przybyszewskis Klavierkonzerte, die dic Zuhörer in eine Art Trance versetzten, sollten die in diese Musik enthaltene Psychose des Entsetzens, heftige Leidenschaften und unbegrenzte Sehnsucht zum Ausdruck bringen. "Przybyszewski spielte unrein" — erinnert sich Meier-Graefe — "es war trotzdem wunderbar".[37] Er "spielte Mazurka von Chopin so leidenschaftlich und erschütternd und sehnsuchtsvoll, wie nur ein Pole sie spielen kann"[38], erklärt Graf Kessler. Edvard

---

[35] Vgl. F. S e r v a e s, *Gährungen. Aus dem Leben unserer Zeit*, Berlin 1898.

[36] F. S e r v a e s, *Praeludien. Ein Essaybuch*, Berlin u Leipzig, 1899 s. 150.

[37] J. M e i e r - G r a e f e, *Stanislaus Przybyszewski*, in: Frankfurter Zeitung 1927, Hf. 876, S.1.

[38] H. G r a f K e s s l e r, *Tagebuch eines Kosmopoliten. Aus unveröffentlichten Aufzeichnungen. 3. Begegnungen mit Malern und Dichtern, zusammengestellt von B. Zeller* (Manuskript des BRD-Rundfunks, J. 1971), Zit. nach F. W. N e u m a n n, *Stanisław Przybyszewski als Gegenstand literarischer Darstellung in Deutschland*, in: Die Welt des Slaven 1974-1975, Bd. 19-20, S. 233.

Munch schrieb über den Eindruck, den er vom Spiel seines polnischen Freundes gewann:

> "Und so tief war seine eigene Benommenheit und mit solcher Meisterschaft wiedergab er die wunderschönen Malereien seines großen Landsmannes, daß er uns im atemlosen Lauschen, fasziniert, Zeit und Stelle vergessens hielt, bis der letzte Ton hinstarb.[39]

Die Attraktivität seiner Person wurzelte nämlich nicht nur in seinem "Anderssein" im deutschen Milieu, sondern auch in seiner Fähigkeit, die übrigens den Polen angeboren ist, sich interessant zu machen. Dieser polnische narzistische Charakter löste bei den Deutschen nicht selten Ressentiments aus. In der Erzählung *Mit dem Falschen und dem ehrlichen Auge* von Adolf Paul wird die Gestalt des Russen, dessen Prototyp der Verfasser der *Vigilien* ist, folgendermaßen charakterisiert:

> "Er war ein Meister in der Kunst, sich interessant zu machen, ohne es zu sein. Denn auf allen Gebieten war er ein wenig Dilletant. Er machte nicht nur in Literatur, sondern auch in Musik, und sogar in Politik. Er hatte etwas von Christus und Scharlatan in seinem ganzen Benehmen, war immer von Glorie des Hungermärtyrertums und des geheimnisvollen Verfolgtseins umstrahlt. (...) Unter unmusikalischen Leuten konnte er deshalb gut als musikalisches Genie gelten — halbgebildete Enthusiasten und literarisch ehrgeizige Damen konnten ihn ohne wieteres als den neuen Messias der Literatur ausschreien. Und in den politischen Kreisen konnte er sich als ein Märtyrer seines Patriotismus, als einen, der jeden Augenblick wegen seines edlen und höchst geheimnisvollen Verbrechens gehängt werden konnte, verherrlichen lassen. Er war also das Muster eines Modeschriftstellers, welcher es verstand, seine Gaben immer bei rechten Publikum anzubringen".[40]

Nach der Meinung von J. Meier-Graefe ermüdeten seine Exzentrizität und die Versuche, die Deutschaen durch immer neue Einfälle in Verwunderung zu setzen, nach geraumer Zeit seine Umgebung:

---

[39] E. M u n c h, *Mein Freund Przybyszewski*, in: Pologne Littéraire 1928, Hf. 27, S. 2.
[40] A. P a u l, *Mit dem falschen und dem ehrlichen Auge*, Berlin 1909, S. 84-85.

"Seine Originalitäten waren neu und reizten uns unbändig. Es lag in ihrer Art, den Reiz, sobald die Türen geschlossen waren, einzubüßen, da man nicht sein Leben lang als interessanter Pole herumlaufen kann. Entweder überlebt der Mensch die Originalität, wächst über sie hianus; das kommt vor. Oder die erhöhenden Taten bleiben aus, und dann wächst der Mensch in die Originalitäten hinein und wird Spezialist; der häufigere Fall. Es liegt auf der Hand, daß so reiche Originalitäten wie die Stachus die Spezialisierung begünstigen, und wären wir damals weniger gute Medien gewesen, so hätten wir diese Wendung voraussehen".[41]

Die meisten Vorbehalte riefen jedoch bei den Deutschen andere Eigenschaften des "seltsamen Polen" hervor: die nationale Megalomanie und überheblichkeit, und eben diese wurden am öftesten in den belletristischen Bildern Przybyszewskis zur Dominante. Dieser polnische Wesenszug seiner Persönlichkeit wurde besonders in den Gestalten Taddäus von Styczinski (*Sozialaristokraten* von Arno Holz), Spiridion Krakuscheck (*Gährungen* von Servaes), Herr Stachelinsky (*Das Liebesleben in der Natur* von Wilhelm Bölsche) hervorgehoben[42], und dem berühmten Polen aus dem Roman von Wilhelm Polenz Wurzellocker, wurde folgende Äußerung zugeschrieben: "Vielleicht sind wir Polen zu etwas Höheren bestimmt als zu Äußeren Macht. Wir sind der Sauerteig, der bestimmt ist, die herrschende Affenkultur in Gährung zu bringen..., das Traumhafte, das Triebhafte, das Mystische, das Okkulte wird emporkommen".[43]

Die von Przybyszewski verbreitete Meinung, daß die polnische Nation die edelste Europas sei, rief bei den Deutschen heftigen Protest hervor. Dieser polnische Mangel wurde von Bruno Wille z. B. als "ironisches Aufbegehren eines der geknechteten Edelvölker"[44] bezeichnet. Das Koketieren mit dem Mythos der geschichtlichen Sendung von Polen, die Betonung der Unterschiede zur deutschen Kultur, aber auch das Verspotten einiger Eigenschaften der Deutschen führten schließlich dazu, daß bisherige Verehrungsobjekt als "Fremdkörper" angesehen wurde. Das so herausfordernd zur Schau gestellte

---

41 J. Meier-Graefe, *Geschichte neben der Kunst*, op. cit., S. 146.

42 Vgl. A. Holz, *Sozialaristokraten*, Berlin 1924; F. Servaes, *Gährungen*, op. cit., W. Bölsche, *Das Liebesleben in der Natur. Eine Entwicklungsgeschichte*, Bd. 1, Jena 1924, S. 370-389.

43 W. Polenz, *Wurzellocker*, Berlin 1902, S. 61.

44 B. Wille, *Das Gefängnis zum Preußischen Adler*, op. cit., S. 187.

Polentum Przybyszewskis führte dazu, daß sich viele seiner ehemaligen Freunde von ihm fernhielten.

"Der geniale Pole" erwies sich für die Deutschen als allzu exotisch und eigenartig. Seine Phantasie und Schlagfertigkeit, seine verträumte Melancholie und Apotheose des Leidens, Fieber und Wahnanfälle, das Herumkramen im Unterbewusstsein der menschlichen Seele und die Verachtung der Wirklichkeit waren — der Ansicht einiger Zeitgenossen zufolge — viel zu gefährlich für den gesunden deutschen Geist. "Wir sollen es sogar möglichst bald vergessen", warnt Franz Servaes, "er ist ein Fremdkörper in unserem Blut. Solange wir unsere "lumpigen fünf Sinne" und unser "lächerlichen Gehirn" noch instand haben, wollen wir sie auch getröst anwenden".[45]

Es besteht also kein Zweifel, daß der "dämonische Pole" in das geistiges Leben des "Jungen Berlins" und in die deutsche Literatur bisher unbekannte Erlebnisse und Werte einbrachte. Das in ihm schlummernde slawische Element des Aufruhrs und der Anarchie sprengte sowohl die literarischen Gattungsnormen als auch die starke Struktur der deutschen Sprache, was kontrovers — wie im übrigen alle Werke dieses sonderbaren Polen — angenommen wurde. Der Ansicht Theodor Lessings folgend ist, "das Adjektiv bei ihm wahnsinnig geworden", und "Przybyszewski würde vielleicht besser polnisch schreiben; die deutsche Sprache verträgt nicht diese farbenfiebernde Unkeuschheit der abgehetzten, exaggerierten Riesenworte".[46]

Diese slawische Art, die deutsche Sprache zu benutzen, fand aber auch eifrige Befürworter. Der junge Kritiker aus Wien, Alfred Neumann, betonte in seinen enthusiastischen Artikeln über Przybyszewski, daß er sich vortreflich der deutscher Sprache bediene: "Man denke nur, ein Pole, der das reinste, oft wundervollste Deutsch schreibt, ein Deutsch, das neue Bilder, neue Worte, neue Verbindungen bringt, die Schriftstellern nicht in den Sinn gekommen, welche in ihrer Muttersprache erzogen wurden".[47]

Przybyszewski war zweifellos eine kontroverse Gestalt in Deutschland. Seine oft betonte Unterschiedlichkeit weckte ambivalente Gefühle: das exotische Slawentum des "sinnlichen Polen" lockte an, das Theatralisieren des eigenen Lebens, eine ständige Maskerade und Humbug, aber auch die nationale Megalomanie stieß auf Abneigung. Für viele deutsche Künstler war er eben eine

---

45 F. S e v a e s, *Jung-Berlin*, op. cit., S. 156.

46 Th. L e s s i n g, *Przybyszewski: "In diesem Erdenthal der Thränen"*, in: Die Gesellschaft 1899/1900 Hf. 1, S. 57.

47 A. N e u m a n n, *Zur Charakteristik Stanislaw Przybyszewski*, in: Wiener Rundschau 1897, Bd. 2, S. 665.

Offenbarung. Wie Franz Servaes bemerkte: "Wer Przybyszewski damals begegnente, war von seiner Persönlichkeit fasziniert".[48]

Der hervorragende deutsche Dichter, Jahannes Schlaf, der nach vielen Jahren den Freund aus vergangenen Tagen wiederzufinden und mit ihm in Kontakt zu treten suchte, vertraute einem Brief Worte tiefster Verbundenheit und Bewunderung an: "Vielleicht sind wir beide Gegenpole (in gewisser Hinsicht): Aber ich kann Dir heute wie immer und immer sagen, daß ich Deine *Totenmesse* liebe und das ich sie für ein großes Meisterwerk und eine Offenbarung halte".[49]

Przybyszewski wurde zugleich zu einer Offenbarung der slawischen Seele, die nach Dostojewski eine weitere Variante des Slawentums, das an der Jahrhundertwende für die Deutschen so attrakriv gewesen war. Eben die Epoche des Fin de siècle, mit ihrem Mißtrauen gegenüber der Materie, mit dem Aufruhr gegen die Fesseln, die das Individuum behinderten, mit einem Interesse für unaussprechbare Gemütszustände, begünstigte die Entdeckung der mystischen und verträumten, irrationalen und voller heisser Spannungen "slawischer Seele" durch die Deutschen als eine für sie interessante Alternative.

---

[48] F. S e r v a e s, *Ein Abenteur des Geistes. Stanislaw Przybyszewski,* in: Neue Freie Presse 1927, Hf. 22710.

[49] Brief J. Schlafs an Przybyszewski vom 11. Juni 1927. Zit nach: L. P r z y b y s z e w s k i, *Johannes Schlaf und Stanisław Przybyszeski,* in: Posener Tageblatt 4. 9. 1932.

Zofia Mitosek — Université de Varsovie

L'Allemand proverbial
(stéréotype éthnique dans la tradition populaire polonaise)

La présence des stéréotypes nationaux se manifeste à tous les niveaux de la conscience éthnique, mais leur fonctionnement dépend du type de message dont ils font parti. Ainsi, les stéréotypes présents dans l'expression individuelle de la conscience sociale, par exemple dans des publications journalistiques, dans des traités historisophiques ou dans les oeuvres d'art ne fonctionnent pas de la même manière que les stéréotypes relevés dans des textes de propagande ou ceux transmis par la tradition orale populaire.

Si l'on compare image de l'Allemand-ennemi, si répandue dans notre tradition nationale, avec celle de l'Allemand tout court véhiculée par les proverbes, on arrive à des conclusions fort intéressantes tant sur le plan théorique que sur le plan historique. Les rapports entre les stéréotypes et la vérité seraient sans doute très intéressants à analyser, mais nous nous proposons d'étudier ici un autre problème qui nous paraît plus important encore, celui des conditions dans lesquelles l'image de l'autre commence à se figer en stéréotype. Cette image, produit de relations quotidiennes, économiques et culturelles avec l'autre, se cristallise en proverbe, revêt la forme d'un commentaire enfin, dans des textes sociopolitiques et littéraires, avec une acception très éloignée da sa genèse.

Prenons ce corpus de textes:

Już to sęk twardy, że Niemiec hardy
1. Les noeuds d'un arbre sont durs, les Allemande sont arrogants.
Niemiec jak wierzba, gdzie go posadzisz, tam się przyjmie.
2. L'Allemand est comme un saule: il prend bien partout.
Niemcze, będziesz jadł kluski? Ja. A z twojej mąki? Nie.
3. Allemand, tu vas manger des pâtes? Ja. Faites de ta farine? Nein.
Pół Niemca, pół kozy, niedowiarek boży.
4. Mi-Allemand, mi-chèvre, voilà l'incrédule.
Zakochał się jak diabeł w niemieckim ubiorze.
5. Il est amoureux comme le diable de l'habit allemand.

Spasły jak piwowar niemiecki /spasiony jak Niemiec.

6. Gras comme un brasseurs allemand (comme un Allemand).

Jasne jak filozofia niemiecka.

7. Clair comme la philosophie allemande.

Przy Polaku i Niemiec się wyżywi, a przy Niemcu ani pies.

8. Avec un Polonais, un Allemand ne mourra pas de faim; avec un Allemand, même un chien crèvera.

Niemcy tylko piją, Polacy tylko biją.

9. Les Allemandes ne font que boire, les Polonais ne font que se battre.

Gdzie Polacy z głodu umierają, tam się Niemcy wzbogacają.

10. Là où les Polonais meurent de faim, les Allemands s'enrichssent.

Co Anglik zmyśli, Francus skreśli, a Niemiec doma nakrupi, wszystko to głupi Polak kupi.

11. Ce que l'Anglais invente, le Français dessine et l'Allemand produit, cet imbécile de Polonais l'achète.

Co Włoch, to doktór, co Niemiec, to kupiec, co Polak, to hetman.

12. Chaque Italein est médecin, chaque Allemand — marchand et chaque Polonais — hetman.

Włoch przed szkodą, Niemiec w szkodzie, a Polak po szkodzie przychodzi do siebie.

13. L'Italien se ressaisit avant les dégâts, l'allemand — pendant et le Polonais — après.[1]

Les textes ci-dessus peuvent être répartis en trois groupes. Le premier (proverbes de 1 à 7) contient des qualifications éthniques telles que l'arrogance, l'esprit de commerce, la facilité d'adaptation, l'avarice. Dans le même groupe figurent des proverbes se rapportant à la religion et à la philosophie. On y retrouve aussi des expansions prédicatives où la dénomination "Allemand" constitue une partie de la comparaison (p. ex. "Clair comme la philosophie allemande"). Le deuxième groupe de proverbes (de 8 à 10) est fondé sur l'opposition entre les Allemands et les Polonais et apporte des qualifications relatives (p. ex. "Avec un Polonais, un Allemad ne mourra pas de faim; avec un Allemand, même un chien crèvera). Enfin le troisième groupe de proverbes qui

---

[1] Nos proverbes viennent de: S. A d a l b e r g, *Księga przysłów polskich*, Warszawa 1889 — 1894, p. 335, 418, 625 (proverbes 1, 2, 3, 5, 11, 13), J. K r z y ż a n o w s k i, *Nowa księga przysłów polskich*, t. 2, Warszawa 1970, p. 603 - 604 (6, 7), O. K o l b e r g, Przysłowia, dans: *Dzieła wszystkie*, t. 60, Wrocław 1961 (12), K. L u c k, *Der Mythos vom Deutschen in der polnischen Volksuberlieferung und Literatur*, Leipzig 1943 (4, 9, 10). Ma communication est fondée sur mon livre: Z. M i t o s e k, *Literatura i stereotypy*, Wrocław 1974.

est constitué de parallèles élargies contribuant à une réflexion plus générale de type "nation — particularité".

Nous partons de l'hypothèse selon laquelle le proverbe est un message fonctionnant dans un système de communication sociale. C'est un texte à double émetteur. Le premier émetteur, ce serait l'auteur hypothétique du proverbe, sujet (individuel, collectif ou anonyme) qui émet une vérité d'expérience; le second émetteur, c'est l'usager du proverbe, quelqu'un qui s'en sert pour évaluer des contextes nouveaux. Le stéréotype proverbial, c'est-à-dire celui véhiculé par les proverbes, apparaît comme résultat de la transformation d'un jugement empirique en jugement de routine, transformation effectuée par des usagers pour qui le proverbe fonctionne comme un commentaire devant apporter la confirmation d'un fait nouveau et non comme la transformation d'une constatation empirique.

Analysons nos proverbes du point de vue de leur premier émetteur, l'auter hypothétique. L'instance en question, c'est évidemment une construction purement théorique parce qu'il est impossible de préciser le moment de la première énonciation du proverbe. Nous pouvons parler seulement de la première version écrite, mais entre cette première version écrite et l'apparition du proverbe il y a une longue tradition orale. La construction d'un proverbe implique son degré d'objectivité. Il serait relativement facile de mettre à l'épreuve des faits les proverbes du premier groupe contenant une qualification directe des Allemands. On peut admettre que la même objectivité caractérise les proverbes du troisième groupe comportant des opinions sur les propriétés universelles des peuples. Ces proverbes portent davantage sur les Polonais que sur les Allemands et constituent une sorte d'autocritique. Bien différent est le cas des proverbes du second groupe dont les textes véhiculent des contenus antagonistes valorisant l'émetteur polonais.

La présence de l'émetteur (du sujet de l'énoncé) dans les textes du second et du troisième groupes indique que ces preverbes contiennent non seulement des stéréotypes d'autres nations mais aussi, de façon plus ou moins apparente, des autostéréotypes.[2]

Quelle est l'image de l'Allemand apportée par les textes analysés? Comment caractériser leur émetteur réel? Ce qui est évident, c'est que cet émetteur, ce ne pouvait pas être un sujet individuel entre ce qui est le sien et ce qui appartient à l'autre est nettement tracée. Cette frontière est d'ordre quotidien, culturel et religieux. L'Allemand apparaît ici comme un partenaire dans le vie quotidienne et comme un concurrent dans la vie économique. Sa religion

---

2 Sur les notions de stéréotype et autostéréotype voir: Z. Mitosek, op. cit., p. 5 - 42 et. P. Hofstatter, *Das Denken in Stereotypen*, Gottingen 1960.

est d'origine diabolique, sa philosophie — du moins ce que nous en savons des textes du XIXe siècle — est totalement incompréhensible, n'empêche que cet étranger n'est qu'on voisin, un peu bizarre, c'est vrai, mais un voisin tout de même, qu'on peut tourner en dérision et dont on peut se moquer. Il est à remarquer que les proverbes sur les Allemands témoignent d'une prise de conscience critique aussi bien à l'égard de l'objet que du sujet de l'énoncé. Les Polonais, avec tout leur paradigme de vertus nationales, ne sont pas non plus à l'abri du ridicule.

Le manque de recul joint à la tendance à la raillerie ne permettent pas de qualifier nos proverbes de satiriques: aucun auter satirique ne s'identifie avec les réalités qui sont l'objet de ses attaques. Une telle attitude — trop impliquée et moqueuse — ajoute une dimension nouvelle à la représentation de l'autre. Cette représentation contraste avec celle, relevée dans d'autres types d'énoncés où le recul, servant à exprimer aussi bien l'hostillité que l'admiration, constitue la base d'un jugement clair, non ambigu. Le groupe qui produit des proverbes avec les stéréotypes de l'Allemand appréhende la réalité à travers "le rire populaire". Ce rire supprime la peur et dispense du respect envers l'objet et le monde décrits, les rend familiers favorisant leur approche directe, presque physique. Il renforce le sentiment de sécurité sans lequel l'approche réaliste du monde n'est pas possible.[3]

La convention du "rire populaire" s'est longtemps maintenue dans la tradition populaire polonaise; elle sous-tend la plupart des proverbes, dictons et chansons ayant pour objet les Allemands. Cette convention, on la retrouve déjà au Moyen-Age, ce dont témoigne cette maxime circulant parmi les Slaves:

Teutonici sunt nati venerunt de culo Pilati;
Poloni sunt tristi venerunt de corpore Christi.

Voilà un quatrain décrivant l'apparence des Allemands:

Un habit étriqué
Les tresses de la perruque pendant sur les oreilles
Le Polonais tire à peine son épée
L'Allemand est déjà mort de peur.[4]

Kusy fraczek, kusy,
Harcapek po uszy,
Polak szablą ruszy,
Już Niemiec bez duszy.

---

3 Voir: M. B a c h t i n, *Tvorcestvo Fransua Rable et narodnaja kultura srednieviekovja i renesansa*, Moskwa 1965.

4 Voir: K. L u c k, op. cit.

Cette attitude moqueuse et constataive n'a pas disparu malgré les douloureuses expériences historiques. Il suffit de feuilleter le recueil "Les chansons interdites" pour retrouver à côté de la très grave ballade sur Hitler ("Le premier septembre de l'année mémorable, l'ennemi venant d'un pays voisin a attaqué la Pologne") des couplets donnant une interprétation beaucoup plus optimiste des mêmes événements:

Hitler Hachę wziął pod pachę
Hitler a pris de bras de Hacha
I se poszli na kiełbachę.
et ils s'en sont allés bouffer de la saucisse.

*

Hitler tak się rozochocił,
Cela l'a mis de si bonne humeur
że i nas o Gdańsk poprosił.
qu'il nous a demandé Gdańsk.
A gdy spotkał się z odmową,
Quand il a essuyé un refus,
Dostał kopa lewą nogą.
il a reçu un coup de pied.[5]

Mais la convention du "rire populaire" n'explique qu'en partie les particularités de l'humour polonais du temps de l'occupation allemande. C'est une convention ludique et le ludique n'est pas propre à la situation de guerre. C'est pourquoi il faudrait examiner de plus près le contexte historique dans lequel se forment les représentations de "l'Allemand proverbial". Les catégories anthropologiques du sien et de l'étranger sont bien enracinées dans la conscience des peuples qui habitent le territoire de la Pologne où les premiers colons allemands s'installent déjà au XIIe siècle: tolérés par les rois, la noblesse et le peuple, ils établissent leur administration, implantent leurs entreprises et ateliers. Jusqu'au XVIIIe siècle, l'Allemand c'est un bourgeois, artisan et luthérien, quelqu'un qui est arrivé en Pologne pour y vivre mieux, pour fuir les persécutions religieuses, enfin pour s'enrichir. L'étranger devient voisin. Ce voisin est différent, il est bizzare, cet étranger, mais il ne constitue aucun danger pour les Polonais. A l'époque, la conscience nationale se ramenait à l'idée que

5 Voir: *Zakazane piosenki,* Pabianice 1945, p. 26.

s'en faisait la noblesse. Pour les nobles polonais, le bourgeois alleman ne comptait pas sur le plan politique, mais il pouvait, tout comme le Juif, se montrer utile. D'où la moquerie et la raillerie, d'où l'accent mis sur les traits physiques, les comportements quotidiens, sur l'attitude envers la richesse et la religion.

La situation change radicalement à l'époque des partages, c'est-à-dire vers la fin du XVIIIe siècle: l'étranger devient ennemi, la différence culturelle revêt des aspects politiques.[6] Pour illustrer ce changement, prenons l'exemple de ce dessin de propagande diffusé sur le territoire polonais à l'époque du Grand-Duché de Varsovie: il représente saint Michel portant le shako des ulhans polonais sur la tête et terrassent un diable vêtu d'un habit étriqué. Pour celui qui connaît les proverbes polonais, le message est clair: le diable, c'est un diable et ce n'est pas un diable, c'est un Allemand, un Prussien. Le dessin annonçait la victoire des uhlans polonais sur l'armée prusienne.[7]

Le stéréotype de l'Allemand actualisé dans ce dessin répond en quelque sorte aux tendances relevées dans les chansons interdites. Mais les conflits armés et surtout l'époque des partages et de l'occupation allemande ont donné naissance à une autre représentation, un autre stéréotype de l'Allemand-ennemi, celui du chevalier teutonique, du Prussien polonophobe ou de l'hitlérien. Ce stéréotype se nourrisait du sentiment d'humiliation partagé par de nombreux Polonais, il témoigne des réactions de défense face aux valeurs d'un groupe ennemi. Notons au passage que c'est à cette époqué-là, c'est-à-dire au XVIIIe siècle qu'apparaît la notion moderne de la nation.[8] L'Allemand-ennemi c'est un stéréotype politique et non plus éthnique comme c'était le cas des proverbes. Ces sentiments d'humiliation et d'insécurité sont nettement perceptibles dans des tract politiques diffusés pendant les Insurrections de Silésie, dans la presse clandestine publiée à Varsovie pendant la première guerre mondiale. Citons ces vers de Jan Brzechwa écrits en 1944 lors de l'Insurrection de Varsovie:

Nic to, że bandyckie hordy
Ce ne fait rien que les hordes de bandits
Opasały stolicę naszą,
ont encerclé notre Capitale
Bo pożary, rzezie i wojny
Parce que les incendies, les massacres et les guerres

---

6 Voir: J. C h a ł a s i ń s k i, *Antagonizm polsko-niemiecki w osadzie górniczej Kopalnia na Górnym Śląsku*, Warszawa 1935.

7 Ce tableau vient de: *Polska, jej dzieje i kultura*, t. 3, Warszawa 1930, p. 48.

8 Voir, T. T o d o r o v, *Nous et les autres*, Paris 1988, p. 199 - 219.

Nie nastraszą nas, nie nastraszą.
Ne nous effraient nullement.
Nie boimy się, nie boimy
Nous n'avons pas peur, nous.
My walczymy o wolność naszą,
Nous luttons pour notre liberté,
Nie zastraszą nas krwawe dymy,
Les fumées ensanglantées ne nous feront pas peur,
Wściekłe zbiry nas nie nastraszą.
Les bourreaux enragés ne nous feront pas peur.[9]

Si les moyens d'expression employées pour décrire ces événements sont différents, si les Allemands sont évoqués en termes pathétiques et pleins de haine, c'est que la vision de l'histoire - et avec elle celle des Allemands — a aussi changé, acquérant des dimensions apocalyptiques. Comme nous l'avons déjà dit: l'étranger devient ennemi. L'empirisme terre-à-terre des textes folkloriques se transforme ici en une attitude refusant aux Allemands toute valeur humaine du fait qu'ils sont Allemands. Dans les proverbes, il n'était pas indifférent si l'étranger était qualifié de gros buveur de bière ou d'hérétique, alors que dans les vers cités, les dénominations "hordes de bandits" et "bourreaux" fonctionnent comme des synonymes. Ce paysage qualificatif constitue l'expression — et non motivation — d'une attitude totalement négative. Mais pour rendre justice à l'auteur de ce poème, il faut dire que ce n'était pas là une attitude complètement dénuée de fondement.

Nous voilà au cœur du problème. La représentation de l'Allemand dans les textes folkloriques reposait sur une observation directe des traits et des comportements particuliers et elle était relativement indépendante des contextes politiques. Dans ce domaine de l'activité langagière, le processus de stéréotypisation coïncide avec une tendance à la rationalisation, mais les attitudes critiquées existent hors du temps devenant universelles. Dans la création individuelle, le jeu de stéréotypisation et d'individualisation revêt une toute autre forme.

II

Bien que le stéréotype articulé par le premier (hypothétique) émetteur et par l'usager réel puisse être identique, l'emploi confère au proverbe des sens

---

9 J. B r z e c h w a, *Pieśń o walce*, dans: Powstanie warszawskie w ilustracji, ed. sp. de Stolica, Warszawa 1957, p. 47.

différents. Si dans la perspective de l'auteur, ce sens est déterminé par les sens des unités lexicales qui le constituent, l'usager du proverbe, l'appliquant à des contextes nouveaux, lui confère un sens métaphorique. Ce jeu des sens, nous pouvons l'observer dans l'emploi des proverbes ayant la structure des expansions prédicatives telles que "Clair comme la philosophie allemande", "Amoureux comme le diable de l'habit allemand". Le stéréotype dont la genèse est purement empirique sert ici à commenter des faits qui n'ont rien de commun ni avec la situation de départ (qui a donné naissance au proverbe) ni avec les Allemands eux-mêmes. Voilà l'exemple d'un tel emploi dans la littérature du XXe siècle. Dans son article *Kilka słów o operetce* (Quelques mots sur l'opérette) (1924) tiré de son recueil *Jarmark rymów* (La kermesse des rimes), Julian Tuwim écrivait:

"Ce spectacle bébête dont la misère n'est que renforcée par la splendeur des décors et la vulgarité des intermèdes devrait céder sa place à la comédie musicale, sans choeurs, sans comtes, sans filles et sans champagne, sans les toilettes éblouissantes de la prima donna (50% des frais et de succès), sans la couleur locale des bords du Danube et du Monténégro, et sans les crétinismes berlinois (du genre "Schatzi, zeig mir dein Fratzi", ou quelque chose dans ce style). Cette grosse Allemande couverte de diamants, cette Rafke de l'art dramatique, il serait grand temps de la jeter aux oubliettes".[10]

Passons sur la chose elle-même, passons sur la germanophobie de Tuwim plus d'une fois manifestée dans ses oeuvers. Mais comparer l'opérette à une grosse Allemande, c'est actualiser le vieux stéréotype fonctionnant dans lee proverbe "Gros comme un Allemand". Les origines empiriques du proverbe ne constituent qu'un point de départ à partir duquel se construisent des sens métaphoriques où la référence aux traits physiques des Allemands n'est qu'un repère purement visuel.

Un tel fonctionnement des stéréotypes est très courant dans la culturre contemporaine. On parle de "l'originalité anglaise", de "l'esprit français" et du "tempérament italien". L'existence d'énoncés pareils témoigne de l'universalité des stéréotypes culturels dans lesquels le premier sens, celui fondé sur l'observation directe, disparaît au profit des sens métaphoriques. Ces caractérisations symboliques et schématiques prennent la forme d'une opposition qui obéit à un code strictement déterminé. Ce code impose le choix d'un type particulier de traits humanis qui permet d'opposer deux peuples sans tenir compte des diversités politiques qui les séparent. Ce choix est fondé sur l'observation directe des comportements quotidiens formant ce que les anthropologues appel-

---

[10] J. T u w i m, *Jarmark rymów*, Warszawa 1958, p. 368.

lent "style de vie". L'aspect stéréotypé de ces caractérisations se manifeste avant tout dans le nombre plus que restreint des traits sélectionnés et dans leut regroupement autor d'une dominante. Une des sources alimentant ce paradigme, ce sont les proverbes. Les stéréotypes ainsi formés ont suivi un chemin compliqué passant de l'observation, de l'induction, du concret chez le premier émetteur pour aboutir à la fonction d'"étiquette" chez l'usager.

Des problèmes analogues aparaissent dans l'analyse des proverbes ayant la forme de phrases complètes. Il s'agit ici de jugements actuels et universels portés sur tous les membres d'une nation. Nous avons ici affaire au même jeu entre le sens littéral et le sens métaphorique. Ainsi, la qualification de "buveur de bière" ("Les Allemands ne font que boire, les Polonais ne font que se battre") trouve sa motivation dans le fait que les Allemands boivent de la bière. C'est le sens littéral. Le sens métaphorique apparaît au moment où l'on ajoute le quantificateur universel "tous" — "Tous les Allemands boivent" et où l'on commence à identifier le goût pour la bière avec le philistinisme, l'étroitesse d'esprit et la lourdeur.Chaque emploi du stéréotype de l'Allemand gros buveur de bière met en jeu son sens métaphorique. La littérature polonaise en offre de nombreux exemples. Voilà comment évoque son voyage en Allemagne le héros du roman de Andrzej Brycht *Raport z Monachium* (Le rapport de Munich):

"Hofbrauhaus. Des hommes GROS. Qu'est-ce qu'ils peuvent être gros! En Pologne, je n'en ai vu qu'un seul, comme ça. Tandis qu'ici: tout un orchestre. Et dans la salle! Tous des costauds, les panses gonflées de bière, les épaules larges comme une armoire, les mufles cramoisis — chandails, vestes, chemises verts et noirs, le peuple bavarois s'amuse! Le vrai peuple bavarois. Non, il ne s'amuse pas. Il atteste ici son EXISTENCE. (...) Gros et robustes, les Allemands chantent fort, liés par le ciment national... Ils n'avaient pas vu les murs et les baraques d'Auschwitz. Ils n'avaient pas vu les bunkers demantelés de Wolfschanze,ce quartier général de Hitler, près de Kętrzyn. Mais il y a en eux le vieux bois des baraques, le vieux béton armé des bunkers. Ils boivent, ils chantent. Chaque jour depuis qu'existe Hofbrauhaus. Avant Hitler, sous Hitler et après Hitler".[11]

Il est difficile de dire si cette description rablaisienne tient du stéréotype ou du vécu. Ce mélange de concret et de schématique, d'images et de persuasion, d'histoire et de propagande s'appuie sur la représentation proverbiale des Allemands.

Prenons un autre exemple, plus intéressant encore. Les écrivains d'avant-garde dénonçaient vigouresement les visions stéréotypées du monde rejetant les rationalisations faites par l'opinion publique, parodiant sans ménagement les

---

[11] A. B r y c h t, *Raport z Monachium*, Warszawa 1967, p. 91.

représentations de la réalité chères aux foules. Stanisław Ignacy Witkiewicz était de ceux qui se complaisaient à braver 'le lecteur crétinisé". Dans son dernier roman inchevé Jedyne wyjście (La seule solution), un des personnages dit: "De nouveau un cours magistral — on ne peut pas parler avec toi — tu t'es gavé de la philosophie allemande et tu dégueules un tel charabia que la tête m'en tourne, tu cognes dans ma pauvre citrouille comme un pic dans un arbre et tu fais la roue comme un paon (...) Toute ta science c'est ce gavage allemand et ce délogé de l'enfer spirituel Idzio Wędziejewski avec son système éternellemant inachevé".[12]

L'Allemand — philosophie, obnubilé par la métaphysique et Erkentnistheorie, rédigeant son éternel Hauptwerk, inventant des Scheinproblem qu'aucune "conception paisible de la vie" ne saurait supporter — voilà le stéréotype de l'Allemand dominant dans la conscience culturelle de l'entre-deux-guerres. Ce stéréotype se réfère en quelque sorte au proverbe "Clair comme la philosophie allemande" où cette philosophie est critiquée au nom de la finesse et de l'esprit français. Witkacy, antichauviniste mais avant tout détracteur de la culture de masse, présente ce stéréotype tout en prenant ses distances, faisant bien comprendre qu'il ne critique pas la pensée allemande mais la littérature polonaise, créatrice de stéréotypes.

Voilà ce que dit le narrateur de son roman:

"Il n'y avait aucune atmosphère intellectuelle — quelques bouffons devenus odieux à force de lécher le cul des foules crétinisées au nom de la finesse déjà purulante et de l'esprit ranci depuis longtemps déjà par suite d'abus (l'esprit vaut mieux, mon très cher, que toutes ces thèses allemandes, très profondes, ennuyeuses et lourdes) faisaient des grimaces immondes sur la vieille préstrade de l'humour national pseudomacabre".[13]

Tout en partageant le diagnostic de Witkacy, tout en comprenant sa méfiance, voire sa haine du stéréotype simplifiant et défigurant la réalité, il ne faut pourtant pas oublier que l'humour macabre des chansons interdites et des blagues politiques (qui, elles, reposent entièrement sur les stéréotypes) constituait un des facteurs assurant la survie de toute la nation.

La littérature polonaise du XIXe siècle s'est plus d'une fois servie du stéréotype de l'Allemand proverbial. Même les oeuvres de cette envergure que Placówka (Le Poste) de Boleslaw Prus, Bartek Zwycięzca (Bartek le Vainqueur) de Henryk Sienkiewicz, Ziemia obiecana (La Terre Promise) de Władysław Reymont ou Wiatr od Morza (Le Vent du large) de Stefan Żeromski recourent

---

[12] S. I. W i t k i e w i c z, Jedyne wyjście, Warszawa 1968, p. 159.
[13] Ibidem, p. 126.

aux représentations de l'ennemi issues de la tradition populaire. Mais il ne faut pas oublier que les stéréotypes-fondateurs de ces représentations subissaient des modifications nécessaires idéologiques chaque fois différentes. La réception et l'impact d'un tel type de littérature devraient donc être considérés par rapport aux sens noveaux se superposant aux représentations courantes. Comparer l'image littéraire avec les produits de la mentalité commune qui la sous-tendent c'est aussi mieux cerner la fonction impressive de l'oeuvre littéraire.